Dump Dogs

The Tail of Milly & Murph

Contents

Chapter 1. Lost and found - Murph. 5

Chapter 2. A visit to the vet - Murph. 11

Chapter 3. Meanwhile in Wales - Maggie. 19

Chapter 4. Passport control - Milly & Murph. 24

Chapter 5. The Road and the Miles – Murph. 31

Chapter 6. Our new homes - Milly Meets Layla. 36

Chapter 7. Making friends - Murph. 43

Chapter 8. Walks with Dad - Milly. 50

Chapter 9. Walks with Mum - Murph. 56

Chapter 10. Agility and Ham - Milly. 64

Chapter 11. Beatrice and Chickens - Murph. 71

Chapter 12. Clever Mother Duck - Milly. 78

Chapter 13. Mutz 'N' Strutz - Milly. 83

Chapter 14. My First Christmas - Murph. 91

Chapter 15. Christmas in Cornwall - Murph. 101

Chapter 16. Milly Versus the Alpacas – Milly. 119

Chapter 17. The Macedonian Mole Hound – Murph. .. 126

Chapter 18. Social Media - Murph................................ 135

Chapter 19. The Rainbow Bridge – Milly. 145

Chapter 20. Sisters in the Ruff - Milly and Murph. 152

A bit about Pawpers in the Ruff. 161

The spay and neuter project. 162

How to adopt a dog. 162

Notes and Acknowledgements. 163

The Route Map. 165

Meet the Gang. 166

Copyright. 167

Other novels by Maggie Jenkins. 168

Sometimes,

it's all about the Happy Ever After.

Chapter 1. Lost and found - Murph.

From the beginning, there were just the two of us. Me and my sister. I am the dark one and my sister, well she is the one with the exotic ginger hair. Life for us began many miles from here, but somehow fate chose to keep us together.

They call us Dump Dogs because that was where we were born. Far away from here where humans are not always kind and where life itself can be very cruel indeed. I barely remember it now, though sometimes when I am lying on my comfy cushion with my head lolling over the edge, listening to the television. Or waiting for the squirrels from next door to taunt me from outside my window, I can still smell it. A dog's nose is like that.

Did you know that a dogs sense of smell is one hundred thousand times as sensitive as that of a human? That's a very powerful thing to own. It can also get a dog into all sorts of mischief.

In my doggy dreams I can detect the aroma of rotting vegetables, rusting tin cans, plastic bags filled with the things that humans throw away, there seems to be no end to the rubbish they create. To many of them anything and everything can be discarded and abandoned. Including dogs.

I can hear the howling and barking of those of my kind who have lived on the dump all their lives and are too old to change their ways. Dogs like my mother and my father. Dogs who will always be wary of humans and will never leave the piece of waste ground just outside the city of Skopje, Northern Macedonia.

My humans have closed the curtains over my window and it is dark outside. The orange of the street light illuminates the front garden. I am sleeping on my perch on a long storage box fitted into the window, I am in my safe place behind the curtains from where I can see anyone who approaches. My tummy is full, meat, biscuit and the remains of the sandwich which my human left on a plate on the coffee table. Silly him! It was filled with ham, one of my favourite things, nearly as nice as the egg on toast I found this morning. My eyes close and my nostrils are filled with the scents of where I was born. I start to dream….

'Sister……where are you, and where is Mum…. she told you not to wander, you were supposed to stay in our den…

I can't find you... ......' I whimper. 'Oh no! They have her.....
the humans with the van, Mum told us to hide from
them.... I must hide.... Stay in the oil drum, don't get
caught. Sister don't stay out there, come inside. They will
take you away..... SISTER......'

My paws tremble and I woof in my sleep, a little, high
pitched puppy woof. In my dream I hide in the darkness. I
am the black one, if I curl up tightly and close my eyes
then they can't see me. But they have found my sister,
and, they have taken my mother .....they have put her in
the van. Don't they know she has puppies? They must
know she has puppies to feed. Now they have my sister....
she must be so scared. I'm hungry and I'm thirsty, and the
humans are looking for me. I curl up tight, nose under my
tail and everything on high alert, waiting. I do not have to
wait long.

'There is another one in here, only a few days old, must
be the same litter.' The human voice is soft and a human
arm reaches into the darkness, a gentle hand grips the
loose scruff of skin on the back of my neck. The people
with the van have me! I should be scared, my mother told
me all sorts of bad things about humans.

'Humans throw things at us, humans put out nasty things for us to eat, meat which will make you sleep forever, the long sleep. Do not eat it…. Never eat it…hunger is a terrible thing, and that meat, it smells so good, your father ate it….. they came for him and took him away and now he is asleep, and he will never wake up.'

That was what our mother told me. Sometimes men come with sticks that make a really loud bang and fire comes from one end, guns, that's what they call them. They fire bullets at us just for fun. Those men come in a big black van with black windows, if you see that van then run and hide, run as fast as you can…. But this is not that van.

There is also a black van which is full of men who come to catch us. One of the old Alpha dogs told us so. He is a dog who is now so sad that he howls at the moon from the top of the dump. He told our mother that they used him as bait for the fighting dogs which the men place bets on in the town. That's how he lost his eye and got all the terrible scars across his once handsome face. He was lucky, he escaped, he ran away, back to the only place he knew, back to the dump. He has no name, the rescue people have tried to catch him but he is too wily even for them.

He has no trust in humans at all. So they just call him Alpha and let him be. He does not eat the food they leave for him, not even the kibble, he will not drink their water. Alpha lives on what he can find amongst the rubbish. One day he knows he will fall sick, and then the big sleep might come for him. Until then he hunts and howls and fights all those who challenge him. The dump is a scary place, but if it's the only place you know then I suppose it must be home.

There they are… in the cage in front of me… my sister and my mother. My tail wags uncertainly and I yap and lift my ears to listen for their reply. My sister yaps back, maybe this will be okay.

I have been a dump dog for six weeks; I have already learned many lessons. Humans come in all shapes and sizes, and despite what our mother says maybe not all of them are bad.

I would not see my mother again, though the humans told me she was okay, she was just one of those too old and set in her ways to start again. I have my sister, we are so small that we can share a cage. That night we curled up together, our tummies full, our bodies warm, the smell was strange, very clean and there was a nice soft blanket underneath us, I close my eyes but keep one ear open, just in case the big sleep comes for me. But in the morning, it has not.

The kind human lady called Marija comes with soft words an ear scratch and my first ever tummy rub. There is a dish of tasty biscuit they call kibble and a bowl of fresh water. Lovely clean fresh water, not flavoured with rust and covered with a slick of old motor oil. My sister is still curled up with me. The kind hand rubs her tummy as well.

'My, these two are cute, I'm glad we found both of them in time, their mother will have to go back but these two... I'm sure they will find homes.'

The kind fingers tickled my chin and I raised my nose and pushed it into her hand. A good feeling swept over me, I snuggled up to my sister and we both slept. Our adventure was about to begin.

Chapter 2. A visit to the vet - Murph.

Always be kind, that's what our mother had taught us. Don't show your teeth, unless it's to chew food. Do bones count as food? I love a bone, the juicier the better. My man human gets them for me from the butchers, really big ones, some still have meat stuck to them. No one is having my bone! Not even my lady human. Was I naughty to growl at her? She wasn't very pleased at the time, but she forgave me. She knows I am still learning the rules and I know that she won't take my bone away for ever. If she does, I still have some hidden away in the garden. But that's another story.

Our next adventure started with a visit to the vet. He's called Ivica. His surgery doesn't smell at all like the dump. It smells of stuff they call disinfectant. Even humans think it smells strong, imagine what it smells like to a doggy nose! It's eye wateringly clean.

Ivica is very firm, but gentle. I allow him to shave a patch of fur from my leg but then he sticks a sharp shiny stick into my vein. Ouch! That's my blood, that's what keeps me alive…. I yelp! I struggle but he holds me tightly so I can't move. I watch as my blood leaves my body and is put into small bottles. It doesn't really hurt and he only takes a little bit.

'Only a paw full.' He smiles and ruffles my ears. 'All over now.' He puts a sticky bandage over the hole. It's not bleeding. I'm still alive.

My sister is still with me. She is being very brave, she's the oldest, but only by a few minutes. I mostly do as she says, but not always. She is like our mother, who was nearly always right.

Ivica puts labels on the little bottles, more new words to hear and learn. He's sending them for testing. To make sure we are fit and healthy and don't have any diseases that humans or other dogs can catch. Then he gets other small bottles out of his cupboard and …..oh no…another sharp spiky thing…. Ivica fills up a syringe with white liquid.

'Just a small injection, just a little jab.' His voice is soothing but it's not just one…. it's one … then another into the skin at the back of my neck. OUCH!

'Don't be silly.' I hear my sisters words, she is being brave. She doesn't flinch a bit. There you are. 'All over.'

Ivica the vet sits us on his table and the rescue lady Marija takes a photograph of us. We are both sitting up and looking at the camera and, if I say it myself, we look adorable.

There are two rescue ladies, Marija and Ivana.

'I'll get this out on social media, these two are really something.' Marija disappears carrying her phone and with a big smile on her face.

We went back to our nice warm pen and our breakfast and waited to see if we were healthy and if anyone wanted to adopt us. We would have to wait for a few months until we were old enough to travel. Until then, we would need to learn to be sociable with other dogs and with humans. We would also need to learn to ignore other animals which humans like to keep, animals like cats. We were growing fast, we would be big dogs, our Dad was huge, and our mother was not small. We could not rely on being small and cute, we were going to be BIG.

Three months passed………Marija started to get us used to people, we learned to sit still….. that's hard. We learn to wear a collar, mine is Purple, it looks lovely on my black fur. Then we learn to walk a bit on a lead. We had more tests and visits to Ivica. More photographs…… we both like having our picture taken. I am the most photogenic! But don't mention that to my sister. She loves the camera as well. We still didn't have names, our new humans would name us once they, like us had been vetted. Pawpers don't just let any old human adopt their dogs.

We had been rescued, we were now Pawpers in the Ruff. We were on a thing called Facebook, where there is a whole community of humans here in Northern Macedonia and in a place called Britain, looking out for us. My sister and I, settled into kennel life and waited.

The older dogs in the kennels chatted to us. They loved to educate the *'young 'uns'* as they called us, about life in the outside world, though hardly any of them had ever had a proper home of their own.

'It's like this, Marija and Ivana will look for homes for all of us, there are whole families of humans who want to look after us, give us what they call a forever home. Marija will check to see if they really can look after us properly she won't let us go just anywhere.'

Some of the older dogs had been there months. A few had been there longer.

'Why don't you have a home yet?' I asked one of them cheekily.

Bruno was only two, he was a chihuahua, when he stood up I could see he only had three legs. One of his front legs was missing. He spoke with a strange accent which I later found out was Spanish.

'Not everyone wants a three-legged dog like me, I am not fluffy and cute. Though I used to be. I used to have a home, I had a human, she was very rich and she carried me around in my own handbag, I had a collar which sparkled with jewels. We used to drive around the city in a big car and go to parties where other humans who also had cute dogs like me liked to drink and dance all night.

Us dogs would all get put in a big play pen like the ones some humans put their babies in. They put us there so we could all play together while our humans enjoyed themselves. She gave me liver and chicken and fed me from her own plate. She called me Bruno. In her own way, she loved me and I loved her. Her name was Marta.

One day I got fed up with being carried, I jumped out of my bag and was sitting on the back seat of the car. I was watching through the open window while Marta went into the shop to pick up her dry cleaning. I saw some men in the doorway looking at her, I could sense that they were up to no good. Marta came out of the shop with her handbag still open, it was hanging from her hand, her coat in its plastic wrapper was draped over her arm and she was trying to answer her phone. She did not see him coming.

One of the men from the doorway distracted her and the other ripped her phone from her hand and her bag from her arm then they both ran away across the busy road. Marta fell over onto the pavement, I had to do something. I jumped through the window and ran into the traffic, I had to get to my mistress, she was hurt. I had to run after the men who had hurt her. I dodged through the traffic and I managed to bite the second man hard on his ankle. He dropped Martas bag and turned and kicked me so hard I went up in the air, all my paws were off the floor and when I landed I was right in the middle of the road. The driver of the car could not stop in time. I heard the squeal of the brakes and then I remember nothing until I woke up in the vet hospital. That was when I realised that I no longer had four legs.

Marta came to see me every day at first, but she was not the same, then she stopped visiting altogether. I was no longer cute. Was it because I had bitten someone, was it my fault. The vet had called me a hero, the nurses said I was brave, but Marta…..Marta didn't love me anymore.

Eventually she took me home from the vet but after a while she left me at the dump. She had a new toy. Another dog called Jasmine. Jasmine whimpered a lot and pretended that I had growled at her. She pretended to be scared of me. She did not want to share Marta with me. The next day Marta put me in my carrying bag and zipped it up over my head, shutting me away in the dark. She put me in the car and had her driver take me away.

I barked for hours but no one came, I had just about given up hope of being found when I heard a van coming. I used what was left of my strength to make the bag move. That was when Marija found me. It was only luck that she had decided to check on the dump dogs that night. If she had not, then I would have died. I had been thrown out like so much rubbish. What a way to treat the hero I was. I hope she treats Jasmine better. We are living things, not toys, are we not.' Bruno was getting upset. He lay back down in his bed and was quiet. My sister poked her long elegant hounds nose into his cage.

'You will find a home Bruno, you will see. At least you have a name! and you are indeed a hero.' She cheered him up, my sister is like that.

We didn't have to wait long for news of our new families…… far away in a place called Wales, things were already happening.

Chapter 3. Meanwhile in Wales - Maggie.

Hi, I am Maggie, I am one of Murph's humans. I remember that day well. The day I made the big decision, the decision to be one of Murph's humans.

It had been a lovely summer, the country had just emerged from a period of lockdown during the COVID pandemic. That had been a really strange time. No one had been allowed out except for very limited periods of time. Those who could, were working from home. Children had been kept home from school and taught by their parents. For the older children University entrance had been put on hold and plans had been changed last minute.

My daughter had at last gone to University in Cardiff. My husband and I had been thinking about getting a dog for months. It would keep us active, be good for our mental health. We had weighed up all the options.

I had owned dogs in the past, I wanted a German Shepherd or a Springer Spaniel. Working dogs which need plenty of exercise. Neither of us wanted a small dog.

It was a Sunday and I was lying on a sun lounger in our back garden enjoying a glass of wine and some chilled-out music from the 1980's. My phone pinged!

I opened Facebook messenger and there was a photograph and a message from my good friend Geraldine. The photograph was of two adorable looking puppies; one was black with a white chest and paws, and tan coloured eyebrows. The other was an exotic shade of ginger with a white nose. They were sisters. They were sitting on an examination table in what was obviously a vets surgery. The message read.

'The Ginger one has a home, the other one hasn't.'

There was no decision to make. The reply was instant.

'The black one is mine!' She looked exactly like the last German Shepherd dog I had owned many years ago. Old Clyde the reject Police Dog who did not have an aggressive bone in his whole body. This puppy looked exactly like him. I was smitten! My next conversation was with my husband.

'Darling! I have found a dog.' I showed him the picture of the puppies on the table.

'Not the ginger one! Please not the ginger one.' I was a bit taken aback, does he have a thing about dogs with ginger hair?

'No, we are having the black one!'

'Are you sure about this.'

'Very,'

'How big will she get, and how will we tell Megan? She always wanted a dog, and now she's leaving home we are getting one. She will think she is being replaced!'

'I'm sure she will love her, she can give her a name.'

'Where is this puppy coming from?'

'Northern Macedonia, Geraldine supports a rescue charity over there. I have to fill in an adoption form and make a donation to the charity, it's all sorted.'

'Can't we adopt a British dog, there must be loads of abandoned dogs already in the UK.' He wasn't convinced.

'We tried that, didn't we, but they always say that we are out of the house too much or that the garden fence isn't high enough. This is the right dog for us, trust me!'

My conversation with our daughter must have conveyed a very mixed message. Meg thought for a few minutes and then announced that the dog would be called Murphy.

'But she's a girl Meg.' I reasoned.

'You said you were getting a boy dog.' And so Murphy it was. Soon shortened to Murph. We would rapidly find out that it didn't matter much what we called her. She didn't listen often. Four years later this hasn't changed much.

The wheels went into motion. A home check on Zoom, some advice about garden fences and access to the front door. A possible escape route. A few minor fixes to our home security and three months later, Geraldine and I made the five-hour drive to Sheffield to collect two adorable rescue puppies.

Milly. Red haired with white bits, and Murphy. Tricoloured with tan eyebrows. Our Dump Dogs.

My, how the two cute fluffy puppies had grown. They were now six months old, gangly with long tails, long legs and paws the size of mechanical diggers. Their looks now betraying their hunting and herding lineage. DNA testing revealed that they were part Segugio Italiano, an Italian scent hound used to hunt wild boar in the forests of Italy. Dad was part Sarplaninac – a large and very hairy mountain dog, bred to guard and herd sheep, cows and goats. They were destined to be very large dogs.

They had both travelled well, they had survived the 24hr drive across Europe together, in fact they had shared a compartment in the van. The driver described them as lovely, clean, and well mannered. After an overnight break in kennels in Sheffield we loaded both into the back of my Ford Focus and began the return trip. We stopped for coffee in the services, but Milly and Murph slept all the way to Wales.

The night we arrived home in the sleepy village of Coychurch was the first night the sisters had spent apart. But Murph was not phased, she settled on the huge blue floor cushion in the lounge and made herself thoroughly at home. The following morning the fun began.

Chapter 4. Passport control - Milly & Murph.

Northern Macedonia

'Have you seen our new passports sister? Ivica and Marija have been writing in them all day.' Millys amber coloured eyes were bright with excitement. I could see the white tip of her tail wagging in the dim light of the kennels.

'Something is happening. What's happening Bruno?' She nudged our three-legged friend into wakefulness through the bars of our pen.

'Nothing for me to be concerned with.' His voice was tinged with sadness. 'Marija will keep me here, this is my forever home. But you…. you are on your way. They have found homes for you, we knew they would'

'Where are we going, Bruno? I don't want to leave here, it's safe here, everyone loves us. I don't want to leave my friends, we are pack, we keep each other safe.' I felt a hollow nervous feeling in my tummy, I didn't want to leave him.

'I have seen this many times,' his wise little voice with its strange accent began. 'When Doctor Ivica and Marija do this, they are checking that you are all prepared to leave. They will check that you have had all your tests, that you have had all your injections, your new family will have given you a name. Ivica will write it on your passport. He will stick a nice photograph of you in the front so that they know who, is who, as if they don't already.' Bruno shuffled himself round in his bed. Then he turned over onto his back with his three paws sticking up into the air and wriggled. Scratching his back on the blankets. Righting himself he continued, unconcerned.

'In a few days the van will come, and you will leave old Bruno here forever. I will think of you all, every day and be happy for you, but it is a journey I will never make.'

'What about Misha?' I asked, 'is he coming with us?'

'Sadly no, Misha is not allowed to go, he has a sickness which humans can catch, he is not allowed to travel. He should have been sent back to the dump but he has found himself a home here. He is a favourite of Marija and Ivica, so they look after him.'

I was sad, Misha was such a lovely old dog. He too had once had a home. For many nights he had entertained us with his stories of the farm where he had lived. His life in the mountains.

'I am Sarplaninac!' He would announce in a long low howl. 'I have job! I work on farm, keep everything safe.' He told us about the farmer who had raised him from a puppy, his mother who had taught him how to use his instincts to herd the sheep into a pen, how to scent the air for danger and how to tell 'the boss' when mountain wolves were close by.

Misha told us about the snow on the mountain tops in winter, when it was so cold in the tiny shepherds hut that man and dog would sleep huddled together for warmth.

'See this coat!' He would proudly shake himself, his brindle fur like a lions mane around him. 'It kept us both warm for many winters. Then one night, it was so cold on the mountain I wake up and find Yanis is not just sleeping, he is dead.'

Old Yanis had no family left, his neighbours took his herd of sheep and goats but there was no place for an old dog like Misha.

'They could not train me to work for them. I only work for Yanis!' He declared. 'I guard his body for three days, I would not let them take him. I growled at them all, they would not take him from me. Then they came with food. I was so tired and so hungry I ate the meat, then I slept but I did not dream, I did not even know where they had taken me. When I woke up they had tied me with a chain to the gates of the rubbish dump outside the town. I had never been chained before, tied yes, but not like this. I could not move, they left me there to die.

Other dogs came, one tried to free me, she was kind, I remember she had bright red coat, like yours.' He looked at Milly. 'She chew through the collar they had put on me. I was free but the other dogs, they did not accept me, there is only room for one alpha dog. The pack leader he tried to fight me, he was a huge dog with a scarred face and only one eye, they said he had escaped from the dog fighting gangs. They had trained him to kill other dogs, he bit me savagely but I proud Sarplaninac, I win fight. For a time I was king of the dump. I father many many puppies, I keep order. Then the sickness started. I think I had caught it from that mange ridden cur I had been fighting with. I get ill, when they came with the van again I was too sick to fight. I ate their meat again and they take me away. I wake up here. They give me the medicine I need to stop the sickness and to keep me well. I think Ivica the vet has a soft spot for me. So here I stay, I am proud Sarplaninac, now I guard the kennels and I will never leave my country.'

Then he had looked at me and my sister in a strange way, head cocked to one side.

'Make this old dog proud, be kind always, like your mother.' Misha retreated to the raised bed at the back of the kennel, he climbed onto it and scented the air, then he howled, a plaintive wail which would be heard for miles. Lying down he tucked his huge head under his tail and went to sleep. We would not disturb him. His dreams would be dreams of the mountain and Yanis. Dreams of when he was younger and his joints less stiff and his coat less grey.

The following day the transport came, a different van with writing on the side and separate cages, room for about a dozen of us.

One by one, Marija and Ivica checked us once more for our journey. Ticking off names on a list as we were loaded. Milly, Murphy, Loakee, Dobby, William, Otis, Charlie, Daisy, Misty, Nela and Nika and of course Bruno....

'Bruno.... Where are you, Bruno...' Marija picked up little Bruno and hugged him. 'Bruno my friend, you too have a forever home.' She kissed him on the top of his head. 'Stay safe, behave yourself, do not run in the road. You do not need to be a hero again.'

She handed the driver a folder of papers, and with enough food and water on board we began the 24-hour journey across many countries to our new homes in Britain.

Milly and I were sharing a cage, it was big enough for two. We were sisters. We would always have each other.

Markus our driver made sure we were all safely shut in and no one's tail was hanging out and then he slid the big side door of the van shut. For a while everything went very dark. Then Markus started the engine and his friend Stefan climbed into the passenger seat.

I could feel Dobby in the cage next to ours shaking. He was terrified. Poor Otis was the same. They both started to whimper.

'Pleeeeease put the light on, open the dooooor. I'm scared of the daaaaark.' Dobby voiced both their fears.

'Hold tight in the back.' Stefan called to us, his voice was comfortingly soft and deep. I heard him moving and the clicking of some switches. Then the lights came on. They were only dim, but we could see each other. Then I felt a rush of cool air as he switched the fan on. 'Is that better? What do you expect, first class bunks and a dining car?' Stefan was trying to be funny.

'Hold tight in the back.' Markus put the van into gear, and we were off. As the van left Skopje, I could hear Misha howling his long low howl, wishing us bon voyage. In the little cage behind the driver, Bruno answered him, sad to say goodbye to his old friend, but happy to be starting his new life. This time as part of a family, not a fashion accessory.

Chapter 5. The Road and the Miles – Murph.

There were twelve of us, all health checked, we must have been tested for every canine disease known to man. All microchipped and those who were old enough had been neutered. That was another word I needed to find out about. None of the older dogs wanted to talk about it. All Misha would say was that he had heard Marija and Ivica talking and that there were just too many dogs being born on the dump, too many dogs being left to roam the streets of Skopje, Charlie and his brothers had been found abandoned at the sewage works. All these dogs just producing puppies every year. Neutering was a way of preventing more and more puppies. More than that Misha thought it beneath his dignity to say.

The van started to move, swaying slightly as it made its way down the side streets and out onto the main road. Dobby and Otis continued to cry and whimper for a few minutes until Markus switched the radio on, and we could hear the sound of a music channel playing through the partition.

We could not see out, there were no windows in the van, the only cage with a view was Bruno's, he was behind the driver and could see through a gap between the partition and the driver's seat. There were windows in the back door, but they were black, so that we couldn't see out. We would have to rely on Bruno to tell us where we were. After all, he had seen a lot of the world from the back of his old mistresses Limo! I wriggled myself around a bit so that I could push my nose between the bars of our crate.

'Hey Bruno! What can you see?' I whispered to him.

'Not much, we are still in the town, settle down can't you or its going to be a very long day.' He curled himself up into a neat sandy coloured ball and within minutes he was snoring.

Our cages were in two layers, Milly and I were on the top deck at the front of the van with Bruno. Dobby, Daisy and Otis were in the crates behind us. William, Pavlos, Misty, Nika, Nela and Charlie were underneath. There was a storage box full of food and water between the cages and the back door.

Charlie and Pavlos were brothers, they were deep in conversation, would they get to see each other again. They lay nose to nose in their crates, desperate to remember every single thing about each other.

'Brother, I will never forget you.' Charlie whined.

'Nor I you, maybe we will see each other again, maybe we will be lucky like the girls have been. They say Britain isn't a very big place, not so big as Macedonia. Maybe our new humans will know each other.' Pavlos tried to reassure him.

'Theres always the socials,' William chipped in. 'That's where they posted all our photographs, humans love to talk about their dogs. I'm sure we will all know what the rest of us are up to.'

'But it's not the same as being together, Milly and Murph are sooooo lucky.' Charlie sighed.

'I hope my humans don't dress me up in human clothes and make me wear a hat or a coat.' I huffed. 'I quite like the feel of rain on my fur, and I don't want to be made to look like a fool.'

'I don't mind at all.' Milly joined in. 'My humans can dress me how they want, as long as I have a nice comfy bed and plenty of tummy rubs. Murph, you really are much too picky.'

'Well, someone has to keep up our standards. Did you see what Marija dressed Bruno up in before she found him a home?' I couldn't help laughing.

Bruno raised an ear and growled. 'It was only a bow tie! Does it matter that it was meant for a clown. It did the job didn't it! Here I am, with you all. I hope I am not going to regret it.' He went back to sleep.

The journey was so long, we thought it would never end. We tried to sleep for as much time as we could. Markus and Stefan stopped regularly to make sure we had water to drink and small meals to keep us going.

Bruno called out the names of the countries as we stopped to cross each border, each new country taking us nearer to our new homes. I never knew he could read so well or in so many languages.

On that first day we seemed to drive forever. Markus and Stefan shared the driving and gradually we all settled down and slept. Every few hours we stopped, in turn all of us were allowed to drink and do our business.

By the end of the first day we were in our overnight stop and Skopje was seven hundred miles behind us. We spent that night in kennels, and early the following morning we were off again.

'How much longer?' Daisy was getting bored. 'My legs are getting stiff.'

'We should be in France by lunchtime.' Bruno grunted from his position up front.

'Oh, my word, what is that ghastly smell! Daisy gasped. I could hear Markus rolling down the driver's window to let in some fresh air, and Stefan turning on the extractor fan. Bruno grunted again and wriggled in his cage.

'I think we had better make a pit stop soon,' Markus remarked, chuckling to Stefan. 'I blame that smell completely on that small dog.'

Bruno may be clever, and brave, but he has some perfectly disgusting habits!

We pulled off the road into a big lay-by and Markus and Stefan let us have our last break before we reached the United Kingdom. When the van pulled back out onto the road, Bruno read out the next signpost. 'TUNNEL SOUS LA MANCHE.'

'That means Channel Tunnel,' read Bruno. 'Next stop London. Only a few more hours and we can all stretch our legs.'

After 24hrs caged and confined to the van we were all exhausted. Milly and I crossed our legs and slept all the way to Sheffield.

We had passed through, Macedonia, Serbia, Bosnia & Herzegovina, Croatia, Slovenia, Austria, Germany, Belgium, and France. That is 9 countries on our journey, as Bruno remarked later, that was an awful lot of signposts.

Chapter 6. Our new homes - Milly Meets Layla.

Hi, I'm Milly, Murph's sister! It's about time you met me, Murph is the chatty one, she talks to everyone, she's lovely, and she knows it. But then she has had to be more independent than me. I had something that my sister didn't have and that was a foster mum! Not the human kind but, our kind, a dog.

Our new owners picked us up after our long trip in the van, and we travelled home in what would be known as Murph's car. We wrapped ourselves around each other and we felt comforted and safe just being together. We fell asleep wondering what was to become of us but so happy that we were still together. Most puppies never see their siblings again when they go to new homes, but we were the lucky ones! Me and Murph together forever! We had both ended up in a village in Wales called Coychurch.

Murph's house is only a short walk from mine, in fact if I sniff hard, I can smell her. Murph's owner and mine are friends.

I was lifted out of Murph's car and taken to my new house. I was sad to be apart from Murph but I soon forgot about her when I saw Layla! She was big and a lot older than me, but I wasn't scared. I ran straight over to her to say hello. Layla just looked at me as if to say, *'who on earth is this whippersnapper?'*

I found out that Layla was a German Shepherd and eleven years old, she wasn't going to stand any messing from a five-month-old dump dog from the other side of the world. She watched my antics as I ran around her excitedly yapping at her with my high-pitched bark. I was so excited I tried to jump on the sofa, but our human had polished it well and I kept sliding off. I spilled my water bowl, I nipped at Laylas paws and in all the excitement I accidentally had a wee on the rug! Layla looked at me like old Misha had looked at us when we misbehaved. She looked at me down her long German nose in a most disapproving manner.

It took her a few hours to realise I was here to stay but when she did, she came over and sniffed me all over then gave me a big sloppy lick. I lay down by her warm paws and she lay down next to me and we cuddled together. I felt safe and loved. As I drifted off, I thought about Murph and had a funny feeling in my tummy. We had never been apart before, and I was going to miss her. I hope she has a lovely new home like me, and I hope I will see her again. Me and Murph together forever, that's how it's got to be.

I already know the noise and smell of Murph's car, our noses and ears are like that. They remember everything. I listened to the noise of the engine disappear into the distance and knew that I would definitely see her again. My human Geraldine had said so and Geraldine would never let me down.

Hi, it's me, Murph, back again. I was there too remember?

The noise of the engine lulled us both off to sleep for hours. I think we stopped but we didn't get out, we didn't need to wee or poo. The music from the radio was different from what we had heard in the van with the other dogs. When we arrived in the kennels in a place called Sheffield, we had watched as one by one the others had been collected by their new families. Milly and I were nearly the last to be collected. But at least we were going together. We howled our goodbyes to the others, and we waited.

When our turn came, we were carried out of our kennel and put into the back of a waiting car, there was a nice soft bed and a blanket and a barrier separating us from the seats. This was my human's car, the car I would go on my adventures in, now it was taking me and my sister Milly home. Home to a place called Coychurch.

I was woken by the tailgate of the car opening and felt Milly being lifted out into the darkness. I was too tired to move. Too tired to ask her if she felt okay. I rested my chin on my paws and sighed. The door shut and we were on the move again but not for long. Then the car stopped, and the engine was switched off.

'Well, Murph, we made it, this is home.' My human was climbing out of the driver's seat. She lifted me out of the back of the car and carried me into the house.

My humans do not have any other dogs, it's just me, but she has had dogs before, I heard her chatting with Geraldine on the journey, so I should be okay. It is dark and I can't see much but they let me outside on a lead to do my business, then offer me some food, not too much but just enough to fill my tummy, and fresh water from the tap. I'm not sure about this water, I prefer mine from the sky, rainwater or water from the river does for me. This water tastes a bit funny. I sneak out through the open door and drink from one of the flowerpots outside. That's more like it! Then, I wander back into the kitchen and towards the sound of their voices. My bed for now is a huge blue cushion in their living room. It's all mine. I don't have to share it.

What do I call them, my humans….? I have a name; they have called me Murphy. Murph for short. I'm not sure I like it, maybe if I don't answer to it they will change it.

My sister is now called Milly, now that's a much nicer name, and she has an older dog called Layla for company. But the old dog is too old to want to play much, she mainly sleeps. So maybe just having humans isn't too bad, more attention for me. I love attention, and tummy rubs, and more attention and tummy rubs. I have a nice new red leather collar with a dangly disc which has my name on it in case I get lost. I don't ever want to get lost, that would be terrible.

My humans seem nice. Her name is Maggie; I shall call her Mum. His name is David but everyone calls him Chesty because he has a very big chest, or Dai which is the Welsh version of David. I shall call him Dad.

I drift back off to sleep with a full tummy and I dream of Milly. I hope her home is as nice as mine. My Maggie human sleeps on the sofa while I sleep on the cushion. The smells are all strange, but the cushion smells a little bit of dog, only a bit, as if the smell has worn off but not quite. I snuggle down and close my eyes, it has been a very long day.

It is early, the sun is just coming up. I've just woken up and I need to wee, I wander around looking hopeful, this place is strange, its lovely but it's not kennels, the floor is soft under foot, not concrete. There are no bars to stop me wandering around, and there are lots of doors, oh dear! I can't find the right door. I've tried several but, none of them seem to go outside……. Oops…. I don't think I should have left a puddle there. Maybe if I just slink off, they won't notice! Oh dear! That definitely got their attention.

Mum is not exactly cross, but she wags a finger at me and shows me how to get out into the garden ………. oh my word it's paradise……. There is grass to run around on and there are flower beds and ……. and there is a wooden deck with chairs to relax in…. Oh …. Do I get my own chair…. please…… I jump up onto one of the cushions and my new Mum laughs. 'Okay Murph…. That can be your chair.'

Gradually we get the hang of it .. I learn where the door to outside is. They learn that if I do a yelpy woof and go to the door, then I need it to be opened. Good…. That's lesson one learned.

    Now, I also have a lovely big crate to sleep in, its huge and is lined with a blanket and has all my toys in. It is my safe space, my den to go in if I feel I need time away from my humans. Mum doesn't lock me in, the door is always open. I think I am going to be happy here. I have my crate and my cushion and my humans. I have a garden to play in and most of all I still have my sister Milly nearby.

Chapter 7. Making friends - Murph.

I have loads of friends in our village, I meet them when Mum or Dad takes me for my walk. I love a walk; it is an excuse to sniff things. I sniff the pavements, the lampposts, the hedges, and the grass verge. I can tell from the smell if another dog has been this way.

Dad calls these sniff-stops the *'dog and bone phone.'* He says it's how dogs communicate and leave their mark on a territory, and how other dogs know who in the doggie world has been there.

I can tell more from one good sniff than a human can from reading a whole book on a subject. I sniff for information, I sniff for danger, or sometimes I just sniff for pleasure. Sniffing is good for my soul; it makes me happy. Sometimes I sniff too much, and Dad has to remind me that we are on a walk. If he pulls my lead and calls me to heel, I leave what I have my nose in and fall in beside him. I was taught to 'Heel' when Mum took me to training classes.

Obedience classes were fun, I met lots of other dogs, some of them were friendly, some of them were a bit nervous and didn't really want to be there. We learned to walk at heel, to sit and stay, and how to turn around on lead without tripping up our human, the trainer used to train police dogs, and he was very very strict. My class also started to learn to come back when we were called. I wasn't very good at that. There was always something more interesting to my nose which distracted me. But Mum is very patient even if she has to follow me until I get to where I'm going, before she can put my lead back on! Man-trailing was much more fun, when I followed a trail I knew I wouldn't have a row at the end, only treats.

Dad takes me out for my walk early in the morning, very early, we go when Mum is still in bed. But by the time we get home, Mum has made my breakfast and filled my bowl with fresh water.

We start by going down through our village and then cross the main road and head for Treoes. Treoes is another village a few miles away. On the way, we pass a friend called Dave's house, Dave works on a farm looking after the cows, when we pass, he is usually on his way to work. His overalls smell wonderful they have the aroma of the farmyard all over them. Dave loves to make a fuss of me so I sit in front of him and then roll over onto my back so that he can rub my tummy, I am a sucker for a tummy rub. Then Dave says that he has to go to work. He usually has treats for me in his pocket. I ask for one by giving him my paw and he gives me a gravy bone. I think everyone in Coychurch carries gravy bones in their pockets. After I had met Dave a few times Dad would let go of my lead so that I could run and see him in his garden. This was fine until Dave left his front door open and I ran into the house and met Daves wife. She wasn't expecting me, but she was fine about it once she got over the shock.

Next, we meet the postie, Sharon, she delivers the mail, she drives a red van with writing on the side. When she delivers the mail she sees me in the window, she must hear me as well because I always bark at her. Sharon also has gravy bones, which she feeds me through the window if its open. I don't bark at Sharon anymore because I know her. I have a list of people not to bark at, they include, Sharon the postie, the window cleaner and Sylvia our next-door neighbour. Oh, and Max who lives across the road with Ronnie my doggie friend. I always give Ronnie a *'Hallooooooo'* howl just to say hello.

Back to Sharon the postie. I recognise Sharons red van, and I sit down and howl a *'Hallooooooo'* at her. She crosses the road and pats me on the head and makes a fuss of me. She chats to Dad who says, 'Come on Murph, or we will never get this walk done.'

We cross the big main road and go down a little lane and then past a farm where the farmer is called Beatrice. Beatrice pretends not to like me, but she does really. She is a proper farmer and not a treats sort of person. If we see her she always says hello. I usually see her on my walk with Mum in the afternoon.

This morning Beatrice is not there but her brother Jim is bringing the cows across the road. We stand and block the road for Jim, I don't much like cows, young cows can be a bit skittish, but these ones do as they are told. Dad says good morning to Jim, and we head off down the lane.

Halfway down the lane I pull Dad to the left and try and take him into a field. This is where me and Mum come on our evening walk. Mum lets me run around and play in the river. Dad is not having any of it, he insists that we stay on the lane. Then I smell a familiar scent. I walk faster sniffing the air, there is someone I know coming towards us, the scent is getting stronger. We get to the finger post and turn right and there in the distance is Trish……. Trish my best friend in the world……. I love Mum and Dad but Trish, well Trish is just the best. Trish should be a dog. She knows everything about us. Mum even asked her for advice about my itchy ear and my sore paw. Trish gave her good advice, my ear is fine now and my paw was just a bit sore from walking on the road. Trish comes from a place called Ireland, she loves horses, same as Mum, and she loves dogs. If Dad sees Trish on the lane, then he waves to her and if there are no cars coming, he lets go of my lead and I run to see Trish. Mum says he shouldn't do this, but I love it, I love it so much that if I see Trish when I'm out with Mum, I try and visit her even if Mum wants to go the other way. I can be quite stubborn about it. But so can Mum. Mum lets me win sometimes, but only sometimes and then she makes me think it was her idea. But I know different. Mum likes to be strict with me but she's a softie really. Trish always has gravy bones in her pockets, in fact she's one big lovely Irish gravy bone. Trish looks after Noodles, he's an old Cockerpoo, I think he belongs to her daughter, she doesn't have a dog of her own anymore. But she has loads of doggie friends.

    Then there's Gracie, she is the same age as me, she is a Black Labrador and lives in Treoes, her human used to work with my Dad. On her morning walk she sticks to the lanes as well. I love walking with Gracie, and if I meet her on my evening walk with Mum, then it's usually in the big fields on the other side of the river. Then as long as the cows aren't in the field we get to run around and play in the river while our humans chat. Mum says Gracie is good for me because when I'm playing with her, I come back to Mum like I should do. I like to show Gracie that I can be like a gun dog as well. When Mum calls me I run straight back to her and sit. Mum loves that and tells me I'm a GOOD GIRL, and I get garlic sausage as a treat. Sometimes it's good to ignore your nose, and do as Mum says, but only sometimes.

Of all the friends I have in the village I think the best is Dexter. Dexter is a Cocker Spaniel, I sometimes see Dexter in the fields by the river with his Dad Nick. Dexter goes to work with his Dad and guards the van. He loves to sit in the driver's seat and pretend to be in charge. Dexter also loves the pub. That's where I first met him, he lies under the table and lets all the children make a big fuss of him. Even Mum says that Dexter is a real sweetie. She has a soft spot for Dexter, everyone has a soft spot for Dexter, he is the only dog in the village better known than me and Milly. He is quite happy to lie under the table and sleep while everyone chats around him. Not like me.

When I went to the pub, I disgraced myself. All I could smell was the kitchen. There was chicken and gravy in that kitchen, it was too much of a distraction, I tried to get in through the door and investigate. Alan the chef wasn't very pleased, he shouted at me and chased me out into the passage, I ran around the pub barking until Mum caught me. Then another dog I didn't know came and sat a few tables away. I tried to make friends with him, but he didn't seem to like me. There was chaos. I tried to drag my Mums chair down the room, I was barking, the other dog was growling. Dad told Mum to take me home. I am much too excitable for the pub. Mum says I just need practice. Dad says maybe we can sit outside in the summer. That would be nice. Dexter says its easy, that I should just chill out and relax, he doesn't seem to have a nose like mine, and he isn't BIG like me. For the time being I will make do with having the run of the house and my Kong Toy filled with treats when Mum and Dad go out to the pub. Sometimes Mum even leaves the radio on for me. I'm becoming quite an aficionado on 1970s music, some humans just never grow up.

Milly and I have been residents in the village now for 4 years, everyone knows us, we are the dogs from the dump in Macedonia. We always say good morning to people we know, especially the neighbours who get a cheery 'Good Morning or Good Evening howl.' There is even a schoolboy who waves at me from the bus. I don't know his name, but he seems to know mine.

We love the village and the village loves us.

Chapter 8. Walks with Dad - Milly.

    Hi, Milly here. I LOVE my new life and my family! Let me introduce you to my brilliant DAD. Of course I've spoken about Mum a LOT, she's my best friend after Murph, but Dad's right up there as a pack leader. I think you would call him the Alpha male.

    His name is Rob, the other members of my pack are 'the kids,' as Mum calls them, so they are a bit like me and Murph – siblings. They are grown-ups really, even though Mum treats them like pups as she still feeds them, so they don't go hungry, and she generally looks after them. Like all good pups they probably should have left home, but Mum says they just keep coming back. Maybe she should stop feeding them. Maybe she just doesn't want them to leave. I don't want them to leave, they always make a big fuss of me, even when I chew their stuff and sit in their space on the sofa.

    Let's get back to my Dad, he's pretty easy going and has a relatively quiet life as long as he does what Mum tells him to. When he comes home from work the first things he does is ruffle my fur, gives me a cuddle and says, *'Hi Beauts!'* which seems to be my pet-name from time to time along with Mildred and Mildew. I want to tell them

I'm Milly, but I now respond to all the other names as well. I'm anyone's as long as there is cheese and a tummy rub attached.

Dad is the early bird of the family, *'the early bird catches the worm,'* he often says to me when he's up bright and early. I find this hard to understand as I've never seen him eating one!

During the Summer months when it's really hot, Dad is usually the one who takes me out while its cool, so my paws don't get burnt on the pavement. I love when it's just me and Dad, as Mum is not there talking to every person we meet! She gets easily distracted. She also says hello to the birds, feeds the horses, says *'good mooooooooning'* to cows in the field, she always chuckles to herself when she says this but I don't really see what's so funny. We always stop and look at the ducks swimming by and she does a little quacking noise. Mum can be a bit weird sometimes.

Anyway, back to me and my Dad. I feel proud and safe walking with Dad as he doesn't stand any messing. I always walk *'tidy'* next to him. We say *'tidy'* in Wales which means that something is good – I think. I strut next to Dad with my head held high and my long nose in the air sniffing as we go. Mum laughs as sometimes she will look out of the bedroom window and watch me and Dad walking down the road as my big fluffy tail swishes from side to side. That's probably the fanciest bit of me and my sister, our lovely tails. Mine is the bestest tail, its bright ginger with a big white blob on the end. Murph's Mum says she knows when it's me in the park or in the field because she can see the white on my tail waving. It's like a big ginger and white flag! Murph's is black and blonde and nearly as distinctive!

    Because Dad's a no-nonsense kind of person he doesn't let me have hundreds of sniffs like Mum does as he wants to get on with our fitness regime and get our steps in. One of the main reasons I like going out with Dad early in the morning is because we often bump into Murph, my sister and her Dad Dai! (that's Welsh for David). We howl excitedly when we spot each other from a great distance and pull our Dads down the lane, it really is impossible to stop the momentum. We wrestle around a bit while Dad and Dai are having a chat. Sometimes our leads get tied in a big knot, it's usually a very quick chat as Dai is always eager to get back as Murph's Mum Mags will have his bacon sandwich ready. Murph says that bacon sandwiches only happen at the weekend, but that her Mum will have made her breakfast and that's what matters most!

Me and Dad usually go for a walk around the same route as it's flat which is great for Dad as he says he isn't getting any younger. On two occasions he has taken me to my favourite place – the Common. I love the Common, it's a big open field with a river and a big muddy pond. The farmer grazes horses there and sometimes the cows are there too. The first time we went I was naughty. Dad let me off lead so I ran off and I rolled in cow pats, then Dad couldn't catch me so I rolled in a few more, they smelled great! It was a brilliant game. Dad didn't think so, he was mad!

He chased me around the field trying to catch me which was so much fun. He caught me eventually and put me on the lead and took me to the river, it was icy cold. He made me jump in anyway to get clean and when I sat down and refused, because I didn't want to get wet, he jumped in with me! Dad couldn't have had as much fun as me that day as he walked home with soaking wet shoes and trousers after his dip in the river.

After a few weeks, the cow pat episode was long forgotten and Dad decided to take me to the Common again. I knew that Dad hadn't really enjoyed his icy cold dip in the river, so I decided against rolling in the cow pats. Dad was in luck, there were no cow pats to be seen, only the wild horses grazing in the sunshine, minding their own business.

Dad took my favourite ball, and we played fetch for a time, and I had the usual river dips and retrieved a few floating sticks that Dad threw in. We had a lovely time, and Dad gave me some cheese and patted my head and told me what a good girl I was and that it was time to go home for breakfast.

Before Dad popped my lead back on, I had to do a call of nature. Dad rummaged in his pocket and got a bag out to scoop the poop. Unfortunately for Dad, while he was rummaging, I was off and running! I could hear him calling my name, but it was just white noise to me. I was having so much fun. The sound of the thunderous rumble of horses-hooves on the ground must have been scary for Dad as they galloped past him, closely followed by a ginger flash of fur. That was great fun for me, and I think it was fun for the horses too but not so much for poor Dad. Dad said I was a bad girl, put the lead back on me and marched me home to tell Mum all about it. Dad didn't take me to the Common again for a very long time.

Dad really is a pushover though when it comes to me. He still loves taking me out, washing my paws and brushing me afterwards and when he makes my breakfast it is always Sardines and kibble. As I snuggle down for the first nap of the day with tired paws and a full belly, Dad gets ready for work. He pats my head before he leaves and says, *'see you later Milly and be good for Mum.'* I close my eyes and drift off thinking how lucky I am, I have a life so different from the one I was born into on the dump.

Murph here, my goodness Milly can talk... did she mention the Common.... I love the Common as well... it's my best walk on a Sunday with Mum.

Chapter 9. Walks with Mum - Murph.

    Nothing beats walks with Mum, I love them so much I know exactly what time we should go out. If she's typing, I go and sit behind her chair, and if she doesn't notice me I push it with my nose so it rolls forward and interrupts her. Then I woof at her and give a little *'come on then'* howl. Then I go and sit where she keeps her going for a walk boots and look at them with my most appealing expression. I nearly always get my way.

    When Mum takes me for a walk we nearly always go down across the fields and across the Common, then she lets me off lead so that I can have a really good run around. On a Sunday we go for an extra-long walk and sometimes Mum puts me in the car and we go to a place called the Smaelog Woods which is a forestry where Mum used to ride her horse when she was young. I don't think she's old now, she doesn't look old, not compared with some of the doggie ladies in the village. I admit she's a little bit older than Millys Mum, but age is only a figure, my Mum is awesome. Dad does nice walks and sometimes we do meet Milly and her Dad Rob but Mums walks are just the best.

Mum does my evening walk, at about four o'clock she puts on her socks and her boots and if it's raining or cold she puts on her wet weather gear and her hat. She puts my treats and tennis ball in her bum bag with the poo bags. She wears the bag around her waist, its dirty and scruffy and smells of all things doggy. Then we go to the top of the street, and I jump over the stone stile, and we wait to cross the big road. Once we are across the road we walk down two big fields, Mum checks to see if there are any sheep and if there aren't she lets me off the lead to play and she throws my ball for me to chase. I do try and behave myself, I know that when she shouts, 'Murph COME.' I am supposed to go back to her and have my lead back on. I'd rather be off lead, it means I can explore more. Sometimes we meet some of my doggie friends and Mum chats to their owners.

There is a lovely lady called Ann, and her dog Brodie and she is usually with another lady called Michelle who has a dog called a Hovawart, his name is Baxter. Baxter is really big, I met him at Steves dog training. He loves to run around just like me, he also likes water and mud. We have a lot in Common. If I meet Baxter, I always get a row for jumping in the boggy bit at the bottom of the field. Then Mum makes me jump in the river to clean up, it doesn't matter how cold it is. Brrrrrrrrr, sometimes it's really icy on the paws. I don't see Baxter now, his Mum and Dad moved away from the village to a bigger house. Maybe they went because Baxter didn't fit in his bedroom anymore, he is a very big dog.

Even if we don't meet anyone, we always have fun. We go through the gates at the bottom of the field and Mum chats to the man who lives in the cottage, he has horses in stables and he and Mum know a lot of the same horsey people. My Mum used to ride racehorses you know. The man, I think he is called Martin has a Dachshund called Dougie who doesn't stop barking. Mum says Dougie has small dog issues and tells him to 'shut up'. He always ignores her! Then we go onto the Common and Mum lets me off lead. Sometimes she throws my ball for me or drags my squeaky squirrel along the floor on a long piece of rope. Then we play tug with it. I'm not really a ball chasing sort of dog. In fact, Mum says I am the worst retriever in the world. Milly is much better at games than me. I will chase the ball but somehow I never get around to taking it back. I'd rather leave it for Mum to pick up and throw again. I know she's going to pick it up if I don't. So sometimes I don't bother, I run off and go and play in the river instead. I love the river game. I jump in at one place and Mum finds sticks and walks along the bank throwing them in then I pick them up and take them back to her. This is much more fun than a ball.

On Sunday morning we go right across the Common and over the wooden stile into the next lot of fields and the woods.

Now, I have a confession to make. When I was a bit littler and still learning that Mum expected me to come back when she called, I did get a little carried away by all the smells in the woods. I have mentioned how I like to listen to moles working, well I also love to dig for …. well anything.

It was Sunday, I was running ahead of Mum following the riverbank and weaving in and out of the trees when my nose told me to follow a smell, I'm not sure what it was, I never found out exactly what it was, but it was an interesting smell. I followed it. I found its house. I followed it away from the river and into the woods. I went through the brambles and leaves under the trees and into the boggy ground right in the middle. I heard Mum whistle, and I did look, and I could see her standing by the gate onto the foot bridge. Then she whistled again. I really must go back to Mum……. Just a few sniffs more, she won't mind, it is *MY* walk after all. Then I found the hole, the smell of whatever it was, was sooooo strong, I needed to dig.

   My front paws began to scrabble at the earth throwing big piles of it behind me. I kept digging until my head was so deep in the ground I really couldn't hear Mum calling. There was earth in my ears and up my nose and it was *WONDERFUL*. This is what I was born to do, my nose was so so happy, I was so so happy, Mum loves me to be happy. Then I couldn't hear Mum calling anymore, I couldn't hear her whistling. I stopped my digging. I was all alone in the woods, I had never been in the woods before, I was lost.

   I shook my head and snorted down my nose clearing the mud out of my nostrils. I was a bit scared, where was Mum? I lost interest in the hole I had dug, I couldn't find what was hidden there anyway. It couldn't be as nice as cheese or garlic sausage. Would Mum leave me? *'Come on Murph.'* I told myself. Use your nose, you know what Mum smells like, you can find her. I put my nose in the air, and I took a big breath in and held it, I let the air run through my nostrils. They twitched as they homed in on a scent, there it was, the smell of Mums boots, they smell of horse and farmyard, a bit like Dave but not as strong, and well they just smell like home. A whiff of garlic and cheese, yes, I can do this. I started to follow the scent.

Mum wasn't where I had left her, she wasn't by the footbridge anymore. I dropped my head to the ground and found the smell of her boots. I followed her trail in a different direction. She had gone right around the woods; she must have been looking for me. Oh dear, this may mean trouble.

There she was, halfway up the sheep-field walking along the fence looking into the trees. Oh, look there is a gate. A wicket gate, I pushed it with my head and made it clang to attract her attention. I sit with my nose between the bars, and I shout 'WOOF.'

Mum was on her mobile phone. Oh no she must be phoning Dad to say that she has lost me. I clang the gate again and I howl for all I am worth and bark at her. 'I'm here, I'm over here, open the gate!'

That got her attention. She's coming back to the gate. Do I stay put or do I tease her by pretending it's all a big game.

Mum reaches in her bag and gets out the garlic sausage. Do I sit like a good girl or do I……. the gate opens.

'Murph SIT.' Mums voice means it. I'd better do as I'm told.

She clips my lead back on and gives me some sausage.

'Good girl Murph.' She ruffles my ears and then phones Dad. 'I've found her, we are on our way home. She's going to need a good wash.'

Oh no, looks like the 'Good girl is going to meet the shower goblin', more about him later.

Mum still lets me run around, but now she knows how to read me like a book, if I show the slightest sign of going on an adventure she keeps me on lead. She is never too cross with me, I always find her in the end, but sometimes we are out for much longer than she wanted.

When we go to the Smaelog woods, Mum keeps me on a long line, that way I can have a run through the trees, but I can't disappear. The Smaelog woods go for miles and as Mum says, 'Don't think about it Murph, I wouldn't find you for days.'

Once we have been across the Common, eventually we come out on the lane where Trish lives, then we walk up a very steep hill and past the old church at St Mary Hill and down the back lane. We stop to feed the horses and say hello, then we walk back across the fields home. On the way home Mum practices my 'Murph COME.' drills and makes me sit and stay and then run to her for a piece of garlic sausage. I can sit and stay for ages and when I'm doing drills I always get it right. It's just when I'm distracted by other things I really can't help myself. Mum always forgives me. I love walks with Mum.

Sometimes we meet up with Milly and her Mum, then we have such a good time, and I stick with Milly, and she sticks with me. We remind each other that we mustn't run off or go missing, neither of us want to get lost again.

When there are two of us, our favourite walk is to get into the car and go to the beach.

Chapter 10. Agility and Ham - Milly.

Milly here! I really do love Sundays! Everyone in the house doesn't leave to go to the place called work, I hate it when my humans go to work as I am left on my own. It's only for a few hours and I'm always okay because I just sleep and dream of fun things like chasing rats on the dump with my sister Murph, nipping each other's ears and playing tug with an old plastic bag. Today I am chilling out on the big couch watching a programme about a man who trains naughty dogs on the television. I love watching the television, especially wildlife programmes.

Mum is in the kitchen, and I can hear the cupboards and the refrigerator opening and closing. My nose starts twitching as I smell bacon and sausages and hear them sizzling in the pan. Dad Rob must be having a cooked breakfast. My nose is very sensitive as I am part hound, actually part Italian Scent Hound, how cool is that! That's where I get my ginger colour from. Mum is doing that thing humans call singing. I wouldn't even call it howling 'cos it sounds far worse than any noise a dog can produce, it's terrible. I don't care as I love everything about Mum.

She gives the best cuddles and keeps my belly full of lovely food.

'Hi Milly,' says Mum, as my nose leads me into the kitchen following the scent of bacon. I sit behind her looking hopeful and dribble on her nice clean floor.

'We are going to agility class today and you're going to have so much fun and there's going to be lots of dogs too.' I don't really understand what this is but Mum is excited so I guess I should be as well!

After a short trip in the car, we arrive at a big place with lots of dogs on leads. I'm so excited my nose is going crazy with all the new smells. There are all sorts of dogs here just like the dump, big and small dogs, dogs of different colours and breeds. Did you know that there are as many as 360 breeds of dogs in the world that's a lot of dogs and an awful lot of poop to scoop! It's also a breed of dog for nearly every day of the year!

After we have done all the bottom sniffing thing and made friends, we head into the big barn. It's really strange, there are lots of things laid out for us dogs to play with, tunnels, walking beams, a see saw and sticks you have to wiggle in and out of. I can't remember what they are called. Bendy poles I think, but I'm not sure. I wait and I watch all the other dogs as they have their turn. Most of them have been before. I must try and do my best not to let us rescue dogs down.

Some of them are very fast especially the farm dogs. I think Mum said they are called Border Collies. If they are really farm dogs then they are not like the farm dogs I know from the dump. Old Misha is far too big and dignified to run around jumping over stuff. These dogs are different, when they see the things in the barn, they bark and yap like crazy and just want to see how fast they can go. The noise is deafening. Mum says that if they are really good at it they get to go to a big competition for dogs. It is in London and it is called Crufts. Border Collies are really good at this thing they call agility. They are so competitive, it's all about the speed, they can't get enough of it, as soon as they finish then they want to go again.

Some of the other dogs are just silly, they keep falling off the beam and some are scared of the tunnel as they have a fear of the unknown. They haven't been left in the dark before.

Now it's my turn, I'm not scared of anything, me and Murph grew up on the dump and chased rats for fun. I wish Murph was here she would really show them how to be brave. I shall have to be brave enough for both of us. Here goes.

Mum walks me to the tunnel and throws some cheese in there, I LOVE CHEESE! I run straight in and Mum calls me out the other side, I run into the dark following the smell and see Mum in the light at the end, there she is, with more cheese…. that was easy.

Next I'm going up one side of a see saw and down the other following the cheese, up we go… I wobble a bit as the slope gets steeper, this is a bit more scary. One paw forward and oooooooh its gone all wobbly and drops suddenly downhill with a bang. I half lie down as it hits the floor. Mum then leads me slowly in and out some sticks in the ground. Just to get used to doing it.

The Border Collies do this at a run, I may need lots of practice. This is a very funny way to walk, I am quite a long dog and it's hard to make my head go one way and my tail go the other, but with my nose on the cheese I just keep going. Now for the last obstacle, it's high and it's scary and my tail is not wagging anymore. It's the beam.

Did I really laugh at that little dog who fell off it, that was mean of me. Oh dear! This is very narrow and dangerous and I have to walk all the way along it to the end, my huge paws are getting in the way. Murph and I have long legs and big paws, my paws are great for running and awesome for digging, but this balancing thing….. its……oooo…. I try to concentrate but all the people and the other dogs are watching me … be brave Milly I tell myself…

Then I smell it! The most amazing smell ever and I know just what it is, HAM!!! There's ham somewhere, my nose starts twitching like crazy and all I can think about is getting the ham. Must find the ham….. where have they hidden the ham…… I need the ham…… sorry Mum…..HAM. The ham is calling.

I jump off the beam and make a run for it and Mum almost falls over as she tries to stop me, she let's go of my lead! I'm free and running around, my nose twitches in the air, Italian ham for an Italian hound. It's over there! My senses lock on to that delicious meaty aroma, a smoke cured, packet of top-quality ham, best before, never mind the date, its best before Milly.

Mum is calling me but I can't think straight. My nose has taken over. People start chasing and trying to catch me, other dogs are barking, some of them daring me ….
'Go on Milly find the ham,' others saying, *'don't do it Milly*

go back to your human.' Everyone is laughing, are they laughing at me? It is okay to laugh at me, but I hope they aren't laughing at Mum.

The scent becomes stronger and I see a bag on a table, yes.... That's where they have hidden the ham...I run towards it drooling. Before I can stop myself my nose is in the bag and there, amongst a lot of other smells is a whole packet of ham!

To a dog from the dump any ham is good ham. This ham is special. I throw the packet up in the air and catch it, I am still running. Nobody can catch me now. I run into the safety and the darkness of the tunnel, it is just like the den where we were born, the old barrel amongst the rubbish. I rip open the rest of the packet and devour it, wow, this ham is really good! I must get Mum to put it on her shopping list.

Now to face the music, Mums going to be so mad and disappointed in me. I peer out nervously and prepare for a telling off. I see everyone smiling and laughing including Mum. I thought I'd let myself and Mum down but it looks like I was the star of the show. I lift my head and swagger a little, wiggling my hips and making the white end of my tail swing back and forth.

'I wouldn't be showing off if I were you.' Mum clips on my lead and we head for the car. We drove home with me tired and with a belly full of ham, Mum driving doing her terrible singing at the top of her voice. I don't think I will be going to agility classes again.

Mum told me afterwards it was ham from Marks & Spencer, she also said that that meant it was very good quality. Nothing but the best for me!

I spoke to Murph later, she has been going to a thing called 'Man-trailing.' Where she is learning to follow all sorts of smells until she finds the person hiding at the end of the smell. Now that sounds like a good job for a naughty nose like mine. Maybe Mum will take me one day.

Chapter 11. Beatrice and Chickens - Murph.

While I'm on the subject I'd better tell you about the day I made friends with Beatrice and Jim's sheepdog Jesse.

Beatrice has a farm, she lives there with Jim, it's an old-fashioned farmhouse, it used to be a watermill and Beatrice lives in only one part of it. The rest is very tumbledown and hasn't been used for years. The farm yard is shall we say, a bit chaotic.

Sheepdogs are supposed to be well behaved and well trained but Jesse is the exception. Jim has been trying to train Jesse since she was a puppy, but he really doesn't have enough time and the farm only has cows for her to practice on.

I was with Mum on one of our walks on the Common and we were exploring the river near to what they call the ford. That's the shallow bit where the cows cross from the field behind the farm onto the Common. I was on my long line – Mum still didn't trust me completely after I disappeared on my digging expedition. We had walked all along the river bank and Mum had decided to trust me off lead for a few minutes and had just unclipped my lead so that I could jump into the deep part of the river and have a swim. I could see that the cows were moving around in the field and then I saw that Jesse was in the field having a herding lesson. They were just finishing training and Jim was allowing her to have a run around and some play time.

Quick as a flash she had run to the gate and under the barbed wire fence and joined me in the river. This was fun. Then Jim whistled to her and like the good sheepdog she is, she went running back under the fence to her master.

Mum shouted, 'No you don't!' and went to grab my harness, but she was too late. I was out of the river on the other side and following Jesse across the field towards the farm. Mum had to crawl under the fence and shouted to Jim to catch me. Jim tried to grab my harness, but he wasn't quick enough. Jesse and I were off towards Jesse's home on the farm yard. This was where the trouble started.

I am part hound, I love to chase things which smell and which run away from me. Like CHICKENS, and Beatrice has lots of them. As I rounded the corner of the barn running in Jesses slip stream, there they were. At least a dozen hens of different colours, some with ginger feathers just the colour of my sisters fur, some with grey plumage and others black. Oh, and a big white cockerel with dark green tail feathers and huge spurs on his legs. A fine-looking bird if ever a hound saw one.

Jesse ran straight through the middle of them without being distracted, they ignored her, they were used to Jesse the sheepdog. When they saw me the stupid birds started to run, in all directions. There were feathers flying everywhere, the cockerel was crowing and the hens were squawking and jumping up in the air, running in circles and unable to fly. I had no choice, my hound instincts took over, my nose focused on that cockerel. I gave chase.

Off he went, running across the yard, through the barn, around the manure heap. I followed, my nose only inches from those fine tail feathers, I leapt at him with my paws, I missed. He flapped his clipped wings and jumped over a wall into the old pig pen. I followed, landing leg deep in manure. Out over the wall on the other side. Back into the farmyard, back around the manure heap.

I could hear Mum and Jim shouting, they sounded angry, Mum sounded more cross than I had ever heard her. Crosser than when Dad came home really late from the pub. Jim was trying to head me off before I did too much damage. Too late. The cockerel had managed to get up onto the roof of the chicken shed, he was safe. But I had seen Jesse, she was hiding in the house and the door was open. I would be safe in with Jesse. In I went, I was covered in well-rotted very smelly pig manure. My huge paws spread it all over the floor better than any mechanical muck spreader. Worse was to come. There she was it was Beatrice! I froze and looked at her and then, I had the irresistible urge to shake, I was wet from the river and covered in pig mess. I shook for all I was worth.

'What on earth is all this commotion.' She muttered as she eased herself stiffly from the armchair where she was having a nap.

'Jesse dog, go Cwtch.' Cwtch is a Welsh word used to tell dogs to go to their safe place. This meant trouble. Jesse headed for her basket with her tail between her legs. She wasn't going to come to my aid!

'Who, on earth are you?' Beatrice was looking at me! Her round slightly weatherbeaten and wrinkled face was wearing a definite frown. She was not at all pleased to see me. She wasn't pleased to see the mess I had made either. Now was not the time to roll over and ask for tummy rubs!

I ran, back into the yard avoiding Mum who was coming in the other direction and Jim who was behind her. Back over the wall and back into the pig pen.

Then I stopped. Above me on the roof was a tabby coloured terror. The biggest cat I had ever seen. Usually cats run away but this one looked at me as if I was breakfast. It arched its back and hissed, all its fur stood on end as it prepared to put a canine intruder to flight. It crouched low, getting the measure of its target, then it pounced, it leapt off the roof of the shed and landed on my head. Its front claws sank into my ear and I yelped. I managed to shake the evil beast off my snout where its hind claws were trying to scram my oh so sensitive nose to pieces. I scrambled back over the wall yelping. 'Mum help me.' This time I headed for the river and back to the village and safety. Mum was on my tail and before I could get to the gate she had rugby tackled me like a Welsh fullback defending the try line and grabbed my harness. I was shaking with fear.

'BAD GIRL Murph! You are a really BAD DOG!' Mum was livid with me. She looked at Jim.

'Sorry Jim.' She said. 'If she has done any damage I will pay for it. This is all my fault.' Jim didn't say anything he was too out of puff. But Beatrice had plenty to say. She shuffled across the yard in her old blue wellington boots and with her hands on her broad hips looked my Mum straight in the eye.

'It's Maggie isn't it?' She said to Mum. 'I know you, don't I, and you should know better. There's no such thing as bad dogs only bad owners. You'll be keeping her on a lead in future.'

Mum looked a bit ashamed of herself. 'Of course I will, Bea. You won't be needing to get your shotgun out just yet.' Mum tried to lighten the situation.

'She is only a pup, she will learn. I think the cat has taught her more of a lesson than we ever could.' Beatrice started to chuckle, then she reached into her pocket and brought out a piece of bacon. It was mostly fat with a bit of meat running through the middle. I never had Beatrice down for a treats sort of person, but it was nearly as good as garlic sausage.

'Theres no such thing as a bad dog is there my lovely.' She ruffled my ears. 'I expect your nose is a bit sore.' She inspected the damage. 'That will teach you, wont it. Don't you mess with my cat.'

Then she looked at Mum and said. 'Mind she doesn't get in here again.'

'I know,' said Mum. 'Theres only bad owners.'

Mum later told me that I was lucky I hadn't caught the cockerel and that none of the chickens had died. If they had, then Beatrice might have shot me! I didn't know quite what that meant, but it didn't sound very pleasant.

Mum hasn't walked me by the ford again, and I haven't seen Jesse since, I think she was sent to the farm down the road in disgrace. I still sit and help to block the road if Beatrice is moving the cows and she sometimes has a bit of fatty bacon for me. Mum and Beatrice get on okay, Mum says she is straight talking and doesn't mess about. I think she's more of a soft touch than she will ever let on. But then, so is Mum.

That's another one for the rule book.

Don't chase chickens and don't tangle with the farm cat.

Chapter 12. Clever Mother Duck - Milly.

   I blame Mum for my love of ducks! In our village there is a stream that has ducks and two of our other favourite walks also have ducks! There are ducks everywhere, even the old farm where Beatrice lives has a few amongst her flock of chickens. Mum loves the ducks, she thinks that they are really cute. The way they waddle along the pavement in front of us, in no particular rush to get back into the stream where they belong. Mum being the chatty Mum she is, always says *'look at the ducks Milly.'*
   Being the well-behaved dog that I am. I do as I am told and I always look at the ducks. In fact it didn't really need Mum to tell me to keep observations on these web-footed residents of the village I have always been fascinated by them and have always wanted to get to know them better. I suppose that is a hound thing.
   On my next outing with Dad and Rhys, I get my chance! Today I am going to Bryngarw (pronounced Brin ga roo) Park with Dad and his youngster Rhys. Luckily for Dad there are no cow pats for me to roll in and no horses to chase so Dad and Rhys will have a lovely, chilled walk with their bestie, ME!

A short drive in the car later and we arrive at the country park and head off on our walk. The sun is shining, this is going to be a great day. We pass the park café and my nose is going wild at the smell of the sausages cooking, I will have one later as a treat, if I remember to be a good girl. *'Behave yourself Milly'* I tell myself.

The first place we pass is the duck pond, all the ducks are sleeping, heads tucked under their wings and a few enjoying their morning dip.

'Resist Milly, resist,' I give myself a reminder.

We head up to the path into the woods and Dad pops me on my long line, I start my adventures sniffing everywhere. There are lots of squirrels rustling through the trees, I gave up chasing them when I was little as I could never catch them. I know my sister Murph has a thing about squirrels, but I know when I am beaten. I leave them alone. There is nothing worse than a gloating squirrel laughing at you from just out of reach.

Out of the woodland we walk in to the wetlands, there are lots of birds here. A little Robin lands on a tree stump near me, Mum loves Robins, she always says it's a sign that a loved one is near, I think of Layla and it makes me sad for a minute. The Robin hops away into the hedgerow. If Layla is as happy as a Robin then that's a nice thought for the day. I will tell you more about Layla later.

We soon reach my favourite place, the river! I love running in and out chasing the sticks that Rhys, our youngster throws for me. Dad used to throw balls in for me but I missed too many and Dad said he's not buying anymore just to watch them float away into oblivion. Time goes quickly as I'm enjoying myself so much and Dad gets ready to put me back on my lead to head to the café and the lovely sausages!

Suddenly I see a duck! Not just any old duck but a mother duck along with her family of cute little ducklings. They are so cute I just have to go and see if they want to play. It will be fun to chase them. They might be the ones from the village, maybe they are here on an outing as well. I must find out! I make a dash for it between Dad and Rhys and hear them both shout Milleeeeeee!!!

I'm so focussed on the family of ducks I forget all about Dad and Rhys. I'm splashing upstream and almost ready to pounce when mother duck decides to fly towards me and past my head, I turn to chase her, this is so much fun. As the chase continues the river becomes deeper so I have to start swimming. I don't really like being out of my depth but I'm not giving up. My ears prick up a little as I hear

Dad and Rhys shouting in the distance, but I carry on with the chase, I am in Italian Hound mode and my nose is in control. Mother duck is teasing me as she's just keeping ahead of me and skimming the water, sometimes she waits for me to catch up and off she goes again. I keep on swimming though I am getting tired now, ducks are much better swimmers than dogs I think. I am now becoming aware that someone is in the river not far behind me waving their hands and shouting! What is Rhys doing in the river and with his clothes on! Silly Rhys! He doesn't look like he's enjoying himself like me and he's waving the lead. Eventually I give up as I'm so tired, I suddenly feel a tug on my collar and the snap of the lead as it clips on, Rhys is saying 'Bad girl Milly!' Oh dear, I think I've messed up again.

Just as Rhys and me get out of the river mother duck flies past giving me the biggest QUACK! …. I guess she's annoyed with me too or is she laughing? Then I hear her again. 'Quack! quack! quack,' Yes she is definitely laughing!

Then I see Dad running around the corner with a red face. He tells me I'm a 'NAUGHTY GIRL.' and *'we're going home straight away.'* We walk back towards the car park with Rhys still wearing his soggy trainers squelching beside me.

Further down the river we hear a lot of quacking and see mother duck reunited with her babies. The clever ducklings hadn't moved. Dad said to mum later that the mother duck had deliberately led me away from her ducklings knowing I would chase her and her babies would be safe. Clever mother duck!

I didn't get my sausage in the end so I won't be going on another duck chase again. I guess I was a naughty girl after all. Rhys didn't come on another river walk for a while, I think it took him all that time to dry his trainers out.

When it comes to investigating ducks. I really can't help myself.

Chapter 13. Mutz 'N' Strutz - Milly.

Hi, Milly here. Me and Murph are always learning new words and new words for today are Mutz 'n' Strutz ……. let me try saying that again just to get my tongue round it, maybe it is really three words. I have a long tongue and some words get in a tangle. Mutz 'n' Strutz what a funny name, what does Mutz n Strutz mean? I haven't worked it out yet but it sounds like fun for sure and I'm going there today.

Mum said it's dog training and we are going there to see someone called Tom. At Mutz 'n' Strutz, I will be learning lots of new things. All of a sudden Mum is being very 'hot'on me learning new things. I like to lie on the sofa, but it's good to learn stuff as well. So it's a place where I am going to learn stuff, Its doggie school. I have an idea what Mutz n Strutz means now.

I have already been on a puppy obedience course when I was littler than I am now and got a certificate too. So what more is there for a dog to learn? I know how to sit, stay, lie down and give my paw which is the most important thing to learn for any dog as it ALWAYS leads to a nice treat.

Mum has to go to the place called work first and as soon as she's back she said we are going to training. I am excited as it means I get special attention from Mum with no distractions. I fall asleep when Mum leaves and dream about me and Murph and our Mum on the dump and our adventures. I wonder if Murph has ever been to dog training and to Mutz 'n' Strutz. It's great when we do things together.

It feels like no sooner than I fall asleep that I hear Mum's car on the gravel outside and the key in the door. I am so pleased to see her and give a little whimper and a howl, Mum reaches down and gives me a big hug.

We are soon in the car and going to the 'training' place, after a few minutes of Mum's terrible singing we drive into a place where there are lots of cars parked. Mum gets me out of the car and tells me to be a good girl and gives me a piece of cheese. I think that's called bribery. She knows that I will do nearly anything for a piece of cheese.

There are lots of dogs there already with their humans sniffing around or just sitting politely. There is a man called Tom, he's the Alpha male, I like Tom straight away and he wears some funny shoes. I found out later they are called Crocs! After I have my wee, we get ready for the training. I really just want to meet all the dogs and do some bottom sniffing but Mum keeps me on the lead. Hopefully the bottom sniffing opportunity will be later. We start our lesson, sitting, lying down and standing up over and over again. I already know this stuff but I carry on as Mum keeps giving me the cheese. This is boring Mum...I know all this stuff already.

'Milly SIT.'
'Milly DOWN.'
'Milly STAND.'
'Milly SIT.'
'Milly DOWN.' I lie down and do my next favourite thing...I need a snooze. I lie on my side and stretch out and give a big huff. I am more curious in what the other dogs are doing.

Then Tom comes over and says something to Mum. Mum is looking down at me playing dead on the floor and laughing! It seems that it's Mum who's not doing things right, not me!

Tom takes hold of my lead, I can feel it straight away, it's just in the way he holds the lead, he means business, I MUST NOT MESS ABOUT. It's Tom.... I wake up and stand up...Its Tom.....I'm all ears, I would listen to Tom without the aid of cheese. On second-thoughts maybe these classes should be called Mum training. Apparently I am a bit stubborn …. That could be the hound in me. Mum needs to be firmer, it's good to be encouraging, but I am not tired, I am just not paying attention. Mum is always making excuses to Tom why I'm not doing things right, fancy trying to put the blame on me, every dog knows we are never at fault it's always the human! There are no naughty dogs, only naughty humans. I wish Mum would listen to Tom as he knows us dogs the best. I think Tom must have been a dog in a previous life as he knows so much about us.

On Sunday afternoon I'm back at training. Extra cheese for me, I'm enjoying this dog training. Tom is waiting for us and has buckets upside down on the floor. I can only think of two things he wants the Mums and Dads to do. Yes you heard it here, some Dads get to go to Dad training too.

One possibility is us dogs need a wash, Is this a lesson in how to have a bath? I know my sister Murph hates the bath. Maybe some of the other dogs need to learn how to behave properly at bath time. I don't need another wash, I already had a good scrub this morning after I rolled in fox poo. Fox poo is lovely and smelly, I have spoken to Murph about it. She rolled in it once as well. It means that we smell like a fox and it disguises our scent so that if we are hunting, any things that might hunt us think we are foxes. It's not that we really need to hunt anything, our humans feed us, but it just smells sooooo gooooood! Humans really don't like it and coating your left shoulder and ear in it will definitely result in a good wash with a bucket of hot soapy water and the scrubbing brush. Today Mum had to get the bucket out to wash me so there's no chance I need another one.

Maybe it's mopping, that's the second thing that comes to mind, mopping! Maybe Tom is going to show us how to hold a mop in our teeth and clean up after ourselves. That's going to be difficult, paws are made for running and digging not for mopping. The car park floor where we train is a bit dirty so maybe Tom wants the Mums to mop the floor whilst the Dads put their feet up and chat about how bad the rugby is. Yes, that must be it, my Dad does that all the time.

The Welsh love their rugby and my Dad used to be very good at it, now he watches it on television and shouts at the players when they are not doing well. C'MON WALES!! Sometimes I join in and howl. Well if Tom expects Mum to mop the whole garage, he may have to buy her extra cheese. Ham won't work with Mum…..she doesn't eat meat! All the more for me says I!

After our collective wee outside and a general walk around to warm up, Tom tells us to go to a bucket. The buckets are still upside down with no water in them. I find this strange and guess that Tom doesn't know how to use a bucket properly. I later found out he lives with a lovely human called Lauren so she must be the one who does all the mopping when Tom is watching the rugby on the TV like the other Dads.

Next us dogs have to put our two front paws on and off the bucket encouraged by treats. It's easy to do though the bucket is wobbly. After a few attempts Tom gets his dog Pretzel to show us how clever she is. Pretzel puts her front paws on the bucket and her two back paws circle around. We sit in awe of Pretzel as she's just brilliant at everything. Now it's our turn.

My paws go up on the bucket and Mum rewards me with cheese. Well-done Milly, good girl Milly, come on Milly, you can do this Milly, try harder Milly! Mum never stops talking in the house and dog training is no different, I think this is the white noise Dad's on about sometimes. Dad just puts his fingers in his ears and laughs. If I put my paws over mine, I will fall off the bucket and then I won't get any cheese. My back legs seems to have stopped working and my brain is just focussed on the cheese it's not thinking about the back end at all. *I want cheese, I need cheese, Mum! where's my cheese!*

Mum says that us girls are supposed to be good at a thing called multi-tasking but I'm not sure this extends to the canine species. After several attempts I'm losing interest even in the cheese. Tom comes over and shows Mum how to encourage me to do it properly. With Tom's guidance my head follows the cheese around and my back end starts moving around the bucket. I think Tom is some sort of dog magician as he always gets the best out of us dogs. I also hear Tom telling Mum not to talk too much to me and only to give one direct instruction, I understand now about the white noise. Maybe I can buy Dad some ear defenders for Christmas!

Its soon time to go home and as its winter time Dad will have the fire lit and my blanket laid out in front of it. Before we left training, Mum got chatting to one of the other Mums and I got some bottom sniffing in. I think that was the most exciting bit about today, sniffing more bottoms and making some new friends. On the way home I drift off to sleep in the car, the training is good for Mum as she is taking Tom's advice about talking too much and she drives home in silence all the way. Dad will be pleased with this new Mum. Maybe I need to re think his Christmas prezzie.

Chapter 14. My First Christmas - Murph.

Hi, Murph here. I have been with my humans for three months now, at least I think it's three months. We travelled here in the Autumn and now it seems to be winter. The nights have gotten darker and the weather is wet and rainy. The leaves have fallen off the trees and Mum wears a big coat when she takes me for my evening walk. It's bright orange with strips which glow in the street lights. Mum calls it her High Vizzy!

I sense that there is something going on, Mum is really excited and Dad is making all sorts of plans. Dad loves to party, sometimes a little bit too much. Partying is a whole new thing for me. I talked to Milly about it in one of our walks together. Her humans do it too. They all gather in one place which is sometimes a place called The Pub, and they listen to music and sing and dance. They sometimes drink stuff called beer, which makes them sing and dance even more. When they have a party, they leave me in my bedroom, did I mention that I have grown so much that I can no longer make myself comfortable in my crate. Mum and Dad have given me a huge floor cushion and a blanket in what they call the utility room. It has a sign on the door which says *'Murph's Room'* and a picture of a dog.

When they go out they put me in there with a bone and my toys. At first I was a bit worried when they went, but just like when they go shopping they always come back and make a big fuss of me if I've been good. So now I just relax until I hear them coming home.

Sometimes I do risk having a little nibble at the door to the shower room. My bedroom is just outside the shower room, in the same room as the washing machine. I nibbled the door just to make sure it was shut and that the shower goblin stays behind it. I don't like the shower goblin, he swallowed me up once and I got all wet and covered in soap. That was a day when Mum was cross with me. I ran off and rolled in some really lovely smelly stuff in the field. It was so smelly that I could hide myself in the smell and try and creep up on the squirrels. I was really pleased with myself. Mum wasn't pleased with me at all! When we got home, Mum fed me straight to the shower goblin! She scrubbed me with stuff called shampoo, then she rinsed me and rubbed me with an old towel and sent me outside until I was dry! Oh dear!

I must remember to add that to the rules and regulations. Don't roll in fox poo! Rolling in poo means a visit to the shower goblin! My sister doesn't get the shower, she gets a bucket wash with shampoo and the scrubbing brush. That must be just as bad!

Back to my story. I didn't understand what was going on but whatever it was, my humans were excited about it. Meg was coming home from university and Mums brother had been on the telephone. I've only met Uncle Giles once, but he's really nice and he loves dogs.

Mum has climbed up a ladder which disappeared through a hole in the sky. I'm not really allowed up the stairs to where my humans sleep. Only on Sunday when Mum has her coffee and toast in bed. Then I go and sit on the bed and see what I can scrounge. I love a bit of toast. With real butter and marmalade. I lie on the bed with Mum and she tickles my tummy. I love that. Dad makes the best toast, with bread that goes really crunchy!

Just outside where my humans sleep, there is a door in the ceiling which must go up to the sky. Well, Mum opened the door and pulled down a ladder. I sat at the top of the stairs and watched. Dad stood at the bottom of the ladder and waited.

I could hear Mum fighting with a monster, then a huge green spikey thing came down the ladder, Mum was still up there, through the sky door, out of sight. Dad took the big spikey thing downstairs and put it right in my spot, the one where I sit in the window and watch the world. I growled at it, but it just lay there. I think it must be dead, I pounced at it and pulled it with my teeth just to check, it didn't move. No, it's definitely not alive. Good.

I followed Dad back upstairs and watched as boxes of shiny balls and stuff called tinsel fell through the door to the sky. Where was Mum, had the sky eaten Mum? No, there she was, she climbed down the ladder with a box of what she called fairy lights. Then she closed the door to the sky. Mum was safe!

'Come on then,' she said to Dad, 'let's get the tree up at least, before Meg gets home. Then we can tell her that we are all going to Cornwall for Christmas.'

'What about me?' I thought. 'What is Christmas? What is Cornwall?' Dad must have read my mind.

'What about Murph, will she have to go to kennels?'

'No, she's coming too, Giles says it's fine and Murph needs to meet the family. She can sleep in the hall and have the run of the garden.'

I could see that Dad wasn't sure, but I so wanted to go with my humans. Wendy in the kennels is lovely, but she isn't my pack and the kennels isn't my home! I started to prepare myself to be good! I must stick to all the rules and regulations! If I do then I will get to go on a road trip.

Mum was busy, she started rummaging through the boxes and bags she had brought down from the sky. It was far too busy for me, so I went out into the garden with my toys, then Dad decided it was too busy for him as well.

'Come on Murph, let's leave her to it!' He put on his boots! A sure sign that there's a walk on the cards. Then his coat and then my lead. 'Come on then, let's go!'

I ran in front of him and sat by the front door, I jiggled the handle with my nose, I love a walk, a walk with Mum is great fun, but a walk with Dad can be just as good.

It's getting dark outside, Dad has his big orange coat on, the one which you can see at night. Mum calls to him before we go out, 'Has Murph got her lights on?'

Dad disappears and comes back with my harness the one which flashes in the dark. 'Does everything have to be lit up for this thing they call Christmas or just me? I'm not sure about the harness, but it doesn't hurt, and it keeps Mum and Dad happy, and I do love my walks. Lights on but not flashing. That's better. Now we are off, up the street, I might even see some of my friends. I have loads of friends in our village.

Dad and I walk up the street and round the corner of the Church. We don't go through the graveyard, that's good, it's spooky in the dark. We make our way past the pub, oh look, it is all covered in lights as well. What is it with humans and sparkly lights, they really can't get enough of them. Oh and look there is a big green spiky thing guarding the door. Is that the same as the one in my window. It is just standing there all lit up. I woof at it, a slightly timid woof, it might move, it might attack me and I'm only young. Mum says I am not a year old yet. I think my birthday is in March. Yes I remember now, Mum said it was on March 5th the same day as Uncle Giles. And my sister Milly. It's written in my passport.

We walk up the lane and across a thing called the railway line. Dad has to stop to check there are no railway monsters coming. The lights are green. When the monster is coming, the lights flash red and we have to wait. The monsters fly past every few minutes, they make a terrible rumbling sound and some of them have really long tails.

Maybe they are dragons, the Welsh love dragons. It's like crossing the big road, I have to sit and wait for the lights.

Dad opens the gate and we are off up the hill. Sometimes Mum takes me in the field just off the lane, lots of dogs from the village go for a walk in there, it's empty, there are no sheep or cows there, they just use it for hay. The farmer says it's okay, as long as our humans pick up after us. That means picking up our poo and putting it in a bag and then putting it in a special bin. That way the ground isn't contaminated by any nasty things in our waste. Our poo isn't like other animals poo, it doesn't disappear into the ground like sheep poo or cows or even horses poo. It may also carry diseases and nasty worms if we have them. Farmers don't like dog poo, neither do non doggy humans.

Tonight it's too dark to go round the field so we go up to the top of the hill and back down the other side and back into the village. All the houses we pass have coloured lights in their windows or hanging like icicles from their roofs, it's very pretty. There are even lights in the shape of a jolly man dressed in red called Santa on the streetlights. Dad says that if I'm good, Santa might bring me a present when we go to see Uncle Giles. But only if I behave myself.

If I don't, then I will be on the naughty list. I don't like the sound of that.

I sniff my way along the wall past the village shop. I can smell Milly! Millys house is nearby, maybe I'll see my sister at Christmas, maybe she will come to Uncle Giles house too. I try and drag Dad down the street following the scent. I'm good at that.

'Okay Murph, we'll go that way.' We turn right towards Millys house and then cross the road. I can hear her, I can hear Milly! Oh look, I can see Milly. Milly is upstairs in the window. That's her watching spot! Her windowsill where she looks out at the world. She's barking and howling at me and, oh dear she's trying to climb out. I can hear her Mum Geraldine shouting at her. Geraldine sounds very cross. I sit down and watch her, I refuse to move for a whole minute. I need to be sure that Milly is okay. I give my sister one of my best '*Hallooooooo*' howls. The ones I save for my bestest friends and my sister. 'I'm still here Milly, we are still together.'

Dad makes me move, he can hear Milly as well. We can both hear Millys Mum Geraldine giving Milly a telling off. Dad is laughing, I think that's a bit mean of Dad, I think humans have a strange sense of humour.

We walk down the side streets towards home. It's been a lovely walk, even though I haven't been off my lead, I've seen my sister, I've seen all the lights in the village and I've learned about Santa Claus.

When we get home our house has lights on as well, Mum has put coloured lights all around my window. And she's moved the dead spiky giant. He is now in the dining room by the door, she has brought him to life with all those coloured baubles, and tinsel and more fairy lights. He doesn't look so scary now. I nudge his bottom branches and tell him his brother is outside the pub. He doesn't reply. Christmas trees don't talk much.

Mum is on the telephone when we get in. She laughs and calls to Dad as he is taking my lead and my lights off.

'It's Geraldine, she says could I tell you to go the other way, next time. Milly has nearly climbed out of the window, she has pulled all the Christmas lights down and she's sulking. She says to ask Murph if she can join them for a run on the beach tomorrow.'

I love my sister, I love my family and I think I'm starting to love Christmas as well.

My tea is in my bowl and I'm sure Mum will let me have something nice out of that big cold cupboard she calls the fridge, later. Maybe some ham, or some chicken. I finish my tea, lick my bowl clean and go for a snooze on my big blue cushion.

Mum has poured a glass of wine and Dad has a bottle of beer. Meg comes home tomorrow, Mum is picking her up, do I want to go too? of course I do! But after we've been to the beach.

Being here with my family is all the Christmas I need. I doze on my cushion with my head lolling over the edge. The smells and the scary noises of the dump seem so far away. But I still think of the others, how are they all, especially Bruno with his three legs, I wonder if it is Christmas in his forever home. And what about old Misha and the others we left behind. I also wonder what this strange place called Cornwall is, Mum is very excited about going there and I think Uncle Giles lives there, so it must be very special.

Chapter 15. Christmas in Cornwall - Murph.

Hi, Murph here. Mum has decorated the house with pretty lights which flash on and off in my window. The Christmas tree is in the dining room, brought to life by coloured balls and decorations and more lights and shiny stuff called tinsel.

A word about tinsel, tinsel really isn't very good to eat. I know, I tried it. I started by pulling a little bit from one of the bottom branches of the tree. I was lucky it wasn't one of the very long bits. I managed to pull it with my teeth, then I held it down with my paws. It was beastly, it wrapped itself around my tongue, the only way I could get rid of it was to swallow. It took ages to swallow, it was like eating a snake, but I couldn't chew it. I don't really know what eating a snake is like, but snakes are longer than worms and I've eaten a few worms which I dug up in the garden. I didn't let on to Mum or Dad what I had done, and the Christmas tree didn't tell on me either, so I kept quiet and waited for the inevitable to happen.

Everything indigestible which goes in at one end comes out at the other. Humans have to pick up our poo after us, unless I manage to hide one in the garden or in the bushes on the Common. I was bound to get found out. I decided to play dumb about it. I ate my tea as usual and sat there expectantly waiting for my walk.

'Sorry Murph, its tipping down, I think you can manage down the garden this evening.' Mum looked out of the window at the rain. I did agree with her, it was blowing a gale and the rain was bouncing off the street outside. I settled down for an evening in, while Mum finished putting clothes into a box called a suitcase, and gaily wrapped parcels into a separate bag. Mum had been busy cooking, she had cooked a huge ham coated with honey and mustard which was wrapped in silver foil and kept well out of my reach.

'I'm packing your bag too Murph.' Mum was putting my food, enough for four days and a new food bowl which had Christmassy pictures around the edge. My long lead and my harness and some of my toys. 'Now Murph you will have to sleep in the hallway at Uncle Giles house, I'm sure you will be fine.'

It was Dad who let me out to do my business later that evening, it was dark and he was standing in the back door with a torch. When he cleaned up after me I heard him laughing.

'Been on the tinsel have you Murph,' he was examining my ever so sparkly Christmas poo in amazement. 'Don't worry girl, I won't tell Mum.' But Dad is awful at keeping secrets, he told Mum anyway. She laughed more than Dad did, after all, it was him who had to clean it up.

The next day we went to the beach, then Mum put me in the back of the car, in my place behind the seats where I can watch the cars behind. After I had had a really good run around, we went to a place called Cardiff to pick up Meg. Cardiff is the capital city of Wales. I didn't know that. Well you learn something new every day.

Meg was really excited about going to Cornwall, she said she hadn't seen her cousins and Uncle Giles for ages, it was going to be fun. We were going off in the car tomorrow and would spend Christmas Eve and the next few days in Truro.

I had my breakfast early and Dad took me for a short walk, it was a lovely day for a change, it was cold and crisp and the sun was shining. When we got back to the house Mum had put everything we needed for four days in the car.

'It's a bit of a squash in the back Murph, you will have to share with some of our stuff.' Mum was loading a box full of bottles into the back of the car, right next to where I like to sit. Maybe she will put the ham in with me, that would be good. Very good, I love ham...

'Meg, please don't put that in with the dog!' Mum read my mind. I could see Meg carrying the ham in a carrier bag. I could smell it…..Meg quickly put it in the front with the humans.

'Sorry Murph. You lucked out there!' Meg ruffled my ears and I lay down on my back and waited for tummy rubs. I love Meg, she does the best tummy rubs, and she always takes a selfie of me when I am upside down.

Once the car was loaded, I jumped into the space left in the back, just enough room for me to stand up and turn round and lie down if I needed to. I was with my family, my pack, I could manage. My humans climbed in, Meg in the back behind Mum, and Dad in the front passenger seat. Mum always drives when we go on trips. Meg had less space in her back seat than I did on the other side of my dog guard. Meg put some music on and we were off.

It was a long journey, but not as long as the one from the dump to Wales. I watched the other cars behind us for a while and then I lay down and let the noise of the engine and the motion of the car put me to sleep. After lots of Christmas songs on the radio and some very bad singing by Mum and Meg, and Dad insisting on having HIS music on for a while, we stopped at a place called The Hog and Hedge.

Mum put my lead on and took me for a wee stop in the special area they have for dogs. She gave me a drink of water and sat in the car with me while Dad and Meg went into the café and bought coffee for all of them. There were other dogs in the car park, all with their cars and their humans. I howled a Hallooooooo at some of them and a few of them woofed back. I think they were wishing me a Happy Christmas. Then a man came over and asked Mum what breed I was and said I was really pretty. I like it when that happens. He asked if I was allowed a treat, because it was Christmas. Mum said I was from Macedonia and that I was allowed a gravy bone, just one though. He gave me two and I rolled on my back and he rubbed my tummy. Well it is Christmas after all. I must learn to howl Merry Christmas. It can't be difficult. I am starting to love Christmas, all the doggy rules seem to be suspended at Christmas.

Mum and Dad and Meg finished their coffee and Mum finished her sandwich and I successfully begged for the crust. Usually Mum ignores me when I wave my paw at her, she waits until I woof until she gives me anything, or she tells me to go 'AWAY.' When Mum says 'AWAY' I know she means it.

Back into the car, and off down the road for another few hours and then we arrive at Uncle Giles house. What a big front door, much bigger than ours. Meg and Dad unload the car and Mum takes me for a short walk onto a patch of trees and grass around the corner of the house. When we get back I get to explore the garden. Its huge!

There are massive trees growing in the middle, some of them have branches which grow over towards the house. There they are, there are squirrels living here, lots of them. Mum has me on my really long line, it's more of a rope really. I spot one in the grass at the bottom of a tree and I charge across the lawn and try and catch it. The squirrel is far too quick for me and scampers up into the branches and pokes fun at me in squirrel language while I jump up and down and bark at him. Or is it her. It's a squirrel, I need to chase it.

Then I explore the house, there are lots of doors, I must not get lost, I must make sure Mum shows me the proper way out so I know how to get to the garden. I don't want to disgrace myself. Aunty Helen is a bit stern, she likes me but she expects me to behave myself, I think she is worried that I might be a bit boisterous with the children who are coming on the day after tomorrow. Helen doesn't like me jumping on her furniture, so I find a place by the wood burner. Mum brings my blanket in and I settle down for the evening.

It's a lovely room, there is a huge Christmas tree in the window. I wonder if he is related to ours and I wonder if his tinsel tastes as awful as ours did. Maybe I shall try it later, but that would be naughty…… wouldn't it?

My humans chat and have a celebratory drink and Mum unpacks the ham, Helen has cooked things to go with it for supper. I don't want those things, I'd just like some ham. My nose wakes me up and I go and sit by the table looking at the huge plate of meat expectantly. I am so absorbed in trying to get Meg to steal me some ham that I forget to go outside to wee. Oops, there's a puddle. Just a small one. On the wood floor. Oh dear, it looks so much bigger than it really is, its really only a small drop!

'Murph, you know better than this.' Mum takes me by the collar and escorts me to the back door. She clips on my lead and I go down onto the grass to finish what I started. Then Mum goes and cleans up the puddle. Aunty Helen is not amused, but she doesn't say anything. Meg slips me a piece of ham from her plate. I do love Meg.

After supper before everyone goes to bed, Aunty Helen makes a big fuss of me and forgives me. 'It's all a bit strange isn't it Murph, never mind you can have a lovely walk tomorrow and on Boxing day we can go to the pub before the family come.'

I spend the night in the hallway, but I am restless, the hall is too big, it's not cosy like my room at home. Mum and Dad aren't where they should be, it doesn't smell the same. I start crying then I howl, I miss my sister and I miss Misha and Bruno '*Hallooooooooo*.' Can anyone hear me. My howl echoes, now that sounds really good, it should certainly wake Mum and Dad. I '*Halloooooooo*' again!

Mum appears from their bedroom. 'Okay Murph you'll have to come in with us.' She drags my bed into their room. I try to settle but it's too warm. I never sleep in with my humans, it's one of the rules I don't mind not breaking. It's far too warm for me where they like to sleep.

Eventually Mum has an idea. She pulls on her shoes and goes out to the car. She puts my bed into the car with the other stuff which smells of me and of the beach and of home, and leaves one of the front windows open for me. This is better, I can sleep here, it's my car it's my bed and it's my safe place. 'Settle down now Murph, I'm not sleeping out here with you.' I settle down. Mum would sleep with me if she had to, but I think I can cope, I'm a big girl now.

In the morning Mum comes and lets me in, I can smell Uncle Giles cooking bacon and making fresh coffee. Mum has made my breakfast and I eat it outside the back door. Breakfast al-fresco, this is really nice for a change. On the way out I have to go through the utility room. It is full of food. How much can these humans eat! And there is a huge chicken. Its vast, and its covered with bacon and butter and smells………..Mmmmm, and it's not even cooked yet.

'That's the turkey, Murph.' Uncle Giles is laughing as he sees me sniffing the air as I pass it. 'Don't even think about it.' I wag my tail hopefully, and Uncle Giles covers the object of my desire with a damp tea cloth. That's a NO then.

The humans have breakfast and then Uncle Giles suggests that we could go for a walk along the estuary. What's one of those, I wonder. We can walk up past the rugby club and down the hill to the coast and then along the footpath to the Heron. We can grab a pint and then walk back. Murph can have a good run around before everyone gets here for lunch.

Off we go, It's a lovely walk down the country lanes and onto the grassy footpath with the river on one side and woods on the other. I am on my long lead, I can see all sorts of sea birds sitting on the water and wading on the mud. Are they on my list of things I must not chase? Probably. I answer my own question.

'Murph, you can't jump in that mud, you will sink.' Mum tells me off when I try and chase a seagull which is waddling down the path in front of us. It flies off across the mud flats and takes refuge with its friends on the water, I start to take off in pursuit. Down the bank I go, and out as far as my long lead will let me. Just a little bit out into the river. Then the grey mud starts to suck me downwards, it is pulling my paws from under me. Mum was right, I could disappear. I scrabble my way frantically to the shore. When I turn back to face the water, I can see the seagulls flapping and jumping up and down. I just know that they are laughing at me! My opinion of seagulls hasn't changed. They are to be chased at every opportunity!

We have a lovely walk ending at a pub called the Heron. Its busy at the Heron and despite the cold we have to sit outside, but that's alright, I prefer outside. I try and make friends with the boxer dog who is sleeping under the next table. He isn't very friendly. He growls at me and I try and run away, my lead is caught around the table and I nearly tip all the drinks.

'She's not quite pub trained yet.' Mum tries to excuse me. It wasn't my fault. That other dog scared me. I sit quietly in my corner while the humans finish their drinks and then we head back for the house.

On the way back Mum lets me chase a few squirrels while I am on my lead and by the time we get back to Uncle Giles house I am really tired, I am also very muddy. Before I can be shepherded through the garage, I am in through the front door and into the hall, spreading estuary mud all over Aunty Helens nice clean floor. Through the kitchen I'm heading for the back door. I'm clever, I know my way. When I get outside to the garden, Mum and Uncle Giles are waiting there with the hosepipe and Dad has an old towel. I get unceremoniously washed off, rubbed vigorously until my hair stands on end, and I am told to stay outside while I dry completely. Well while I am drying I'd just as well explore a bit. This garden is awesome, there are all sorts of places to dig and some lovely corners in which to stick my nose, and in all the commotion Dad has forgotten to put me back on my rope.

I think I heard Mum say that she was getting in the shower, Dad and Uncle Giles are making things called cocktails in the big open plan lounge and Meg is helping Aunty Helen set the table. Dinner is in a few hours and the rest of the family are due soon. Christmas is a big thing for human families. I will get to meet loads of new humans, some of them are human puppies. Very small, and I must be really gentle with them. I remember that Misha and my doggie mother said I must always be nice. While they are all busy I check out the strange see-through house in the corner of the garden. It seems to have lots of broken panes of glass and its full of old flower pots and gardening stuff. It reminds me of the dump.

What's this, I stick my nose through a hole in the fence. Oh look, there is another big garden, and another house with more humans, I can hear them, maybe I ought to go and make friends. I put my front paws through and wiggle a bit, I'm through. I trot across the grass and up to the open doorway of the house to introduce myself. I sit politely at the door and howl 'Hallooooooo' then the smell hits my nose. Turkey! and ham…… on a plate. I can't help myself. I let myself in before the humans realise I'm there, and I jump up and put my paws on the kitchen counter. This is not allowed at home, Milly says it's not allowed in her home either. It is a big NO NO.

I have just taken the corner of the big piece of foil delicately in my teeth and am lifting it to check which of the delicacies is hidden there, when, I hear the door open.

'Mum! there's a dog in the kitchen.' It's a boy, he's not as big as Millys boy humans, he's the same size as my friend on the school bus. Maybe he's a friend. I sit, and look at him with my best appealing puppy eyes. 'Mum she's gorgeous. Look she's begging.' I am now waving my paw at him. His Mum is not so sure.

'Julian, where did she come from. None of the neighbours has a dog. I hope she hasn't stolen the meat.'

Julians Mum is frantically checking the silver foil coverings of the plates. Then she spots a telltale pawprint on the worktop. I make a dive for the door back into the garden followed by Julian. I head for the hole in the fence but I can't get back through. Why are some holes like that? One way only. I feel a strong hand on my collar, it's not Julian, it's his father Alan.

'I think she must be from Mr Morgans house, I think I heard a dog there yesterday. I'll take her back. I haven't met Mr Morgan yet. Christmas Day seems a good time.'

He looped an old belt through my collar and walked me in disgrace back to Uncle Giles house. He knocked the door and waited. I could hear Mum in the shower. I heard Uncle Giles answer the door and Alan asking. 'Have you lost a dog?'

'Come in, come in.' Uncle Giles is very hospitable. 'Yes, that's Murph, she belongs to my sister and her family. Dai! take the dog off this man.'

'I'm Alan,' the man holds out his hand. 'We live in the house behind, moved in last month. I don't think we've met yet.' Alan introduced himself.

'Merry Christmas, come in, sorry about the dog, hope she didn't eat anything. I really should have fixed that hole in the corner. Would you like a glass of fizz!' Uncle Giles the genial host saves the day.

Then Mum appeared wearing her best clothes, she took me to one side and wiped my paws and gave me a brush.

Alan finished his glass of fizz and left, chuckling about the whole thing. I hadn't eaten or stolen anything, no harm done. I spent the rest of the afternoon on my blanket by the fire. I met Megans cousins and their children and I lay there and had my tummy rubbed and thoroughly enjoyed myself. I went for a run round the garden at tea time, well supervised by the older children.

Just after tea, the family sat down and handed out all the parcels under the Christmas tree, presents for everyone including me. I got a new Squeaky Squirrel and a big ham bone to chew. The naughty list must be very hard to get onto.

'Millys got a Christmas jumper, you got off lightly Murph.' Mum knows I won't wear stuff.

She showed me a picture Geraldine had sent of my sister looking rather silly in a patterned jumper with a reindeers nose on the front, and a pink tutu. She also had reindeer antlers fixed to her head. Someone needs to tell her that pink voile just doesn't go with ginger fur.

In the evening Mum took me for a short walk around the block. That night I slept in my impromptu crate in the car, I slept like a log. It had been an interesting day.

The next day we went out in the car, we went to a huge beach. It was another crisp day and the beach was crowded with people and dogs. I didn't say hello to any strangers though one lovely lady said how pretty I was. I was so good that Mum let me run off lead for a bit. I went all the way down to the sea. The sea was huge, much bigger waves than we get in Wales. I jumped in the surf and had a swim and another man asked what breed I was and said I was lovely. I wagged my tail at him and howled at him and he laughed. I think I made more friends, it's good to make friends.

On the way back to Uncle Giles house we stopped in a tiny pub and I curled up under the table. I'm learning how to be a pub dog. It's not so difficult if I really try hard. I try and remember the good advice my friend Dexter gave me. *'Ignore the food, and don't drag the furniture!'*

In the afternoon, Aunty Helens family were visiting and I was on best behaviour. The afternoon passed without incident, the adult humans played games and Uncle Giles played his guitar and sang some songs. He's a much better singer than Mum and he plays the guitar really well, I didn't need to fill in any notes or sing along with the chorus.

In the morning it was time to pack the car and go back to Wales. While Mum was collecting our belongings up, I went on another explore. I had heard Uncle Giles say that the squirrels sometimes got very cheeky and came right into his study upstairs. I think I'd better check, there may be a cheeky squirrel there now.

I crept up the stairs. Round the corner. No squirrels, but there were funny looking birds, made of tinsel and wire and with silly boggly eyes. There were three of them. Why don't they run away? They should run away. I barked at one. It just boggled its eyes at me and didn't say anything. I pounced at it. It didn't move. I had it, it was in my mouth, I held it down with both of my paws and I swallowed. Oh dear, that was another mouthful of tinsel and look, its eyes are missing. I ran down the stairs with it, shaking it hard.

Then back up the stairs, this was fun. I imagined it fighting back and threw it in the air and fought with it. Then I heard the shout from downstairs.

It was Aunty Helen. 'Has anyone seen Murph, I hope she hasn't gone visiting again.'

Then I heard footsteps on the stairs, I recognised them as Mum. Mum was holding something in her hand. I slunk into Uncle Giles study. I took the remains of my quarry and hid under the big desk. Mum shook her head.

'What have you done Murph?' She held up a piece of wire with a boggle eye on the end. 'Where is the rest of it?'

I could only give her my best '*I couldn't help it.*' look. The one where I hide my nose under my paws and raise my eyebrows.

Aunty Helen had three very special Christmas ornaments, she had owned them for many years. They were of great sentimental value. They were a family of three tinsel and wire penguins. They had sat on the stairs every Christmas for twenty years. Now, thanks to my superior hunting skills, there were only two.

Mum bought Aunty Helen a new Penguin ornament to hang on the tree. One from all of us with the date on it and our names. It was a Christmas she would never forget. I was really sorry I had killed her biggest penguin.

I was sad to go, I like Cornwall, maybe I can come again. Perhaps when I have learned to behave myself better.

Aunty Helen says that when I'm older and I have calmed down a bit she may allow me back, but until then, if Mum goes to see Uncle Giles in Cornwall I get to go to Wendys.

Maybe next year!

Chapter 16. Milly Versus the Alpacas – Milly.

Hi, Milly here. Its Wednesday and its Mum and Dad's day off, that is when they don't go to the 'work' place and usually take me somewhere exciting.

'Let's go visit Uncle Craig & Aunt Julie and your cousins at their farm in West Wales.' Mum was doing her excited dance again. That usually means a trip in the car, with singing and an adventure. 'They have some new animal friends for you to see.'

As long as I don't have to perform tricks on a bucket again, I'm up for a day out!

Mum is excited to go on a road trip. I also love a road trip! I sit in the back of the car and Dad puts the window down so I can put my nose out for sniffs. I love the feeling of my ears flapping around in the wind. An hour later we are at the farm. I just can't contain my excitement and start howling to let my doggie cousins know I've arrived.

As soon as we pull up I see my youngest cousin Reicher! His big giant black schnauzer head is through the dog flap at the bottom of the door, silly dog! As I jump out of the car the front door is opened and out comes Dexter, he's a Goldendoodle and just as silly as Reicher. That's a different Dexter from Murph's friend the Spaniel.

I'm not a small dog as I am part mountain dog but I feel small next to my boy cousins. I am so excited I have to run to the grass and do a BIG girl wee, Dexter and Reicher go crazy and do wees too! What is it with excitement, it always makes me want to wee myself.

The humans let us run riot for a few minutes and we all chase each other around the farm and jump on top of each other, this is the only time I feel submissive so I lie on my back on the ground, this actually calms the boys down for a few seconds and then I am up and running again with the boys chasing me.

There are so many places to explore! Mum said Uncle Craig has 33 acres, that's a lot of land. There are foxes, badgers, rabbits and mice here but you have to be up very early in the morning to see them. If there are foxes then maybe there is fox poo to roll in. I wonder if Uncle Craig has a bucket and a scrubbing brush, just in case.

We all go for a walk around the farm and head for a place called the swimming hole, us dogs love it here, we can mess around and get mucky as there isn't a lot of water in there so it's more like a mud bath. Dexter is not so golden after a roll here, he is as black as his brother Reicher. I like this farm life, I can get as dirty as I like and no one seems to be looking for the shampoo.

We all feel a bit tired after our long walk so we head back to the farm. Aunt Julie says 'lets go see our new arrivals.... They are called alpacas! I've never heard of them before, I wonder what they will look like.

We all walk back towards the farmhouse and head towards a small field with a stone barn. This is where the Alpacas live, their names are Rusty, Oreo and Casper. We wait by the gate and peer through and Aunt Julie calls their names, one by one they pop their heads out of the barn and look at us looking back at them. Slowly they venture out and I can't believe what I am seeing, they don't look anything like us dogs. They are BIG, with long necks, funny teeth and they are very woolly a bit like a cross between a sheep and a giraffe. I've seen a giraffe on a wildlife programme presented by that wonderful Mr Attenborough.

I howl at them to say 'Hi' but they look frightened and just stand still. I think they are scared as they haven't seen me before. I howl again and put my head through the gate to get closer, they move back and just stare at me. They are no fun at all, not like Dexter and Reicher. What do alpacas actually do, they don't seem to move much, and they aren't very talkative.

Aunt Julie opens the gate and goes into check their food and water with mum. My doggie cousins have seen it all before so head back to the farmhouse with Dad and Uncle Craig for food, but not me, I am fixated on the silly alpacas. I need to find out more about them, maybe they just don't understand me. Maybe they speak a different language. I think I saw a programme on the telly once which was about Peru. I think it said that alpacas were from Peru. Maybe they speak like Paddington Bear, he was from darkest Peru. I wonder if they like Marmalade Sandwiches too. My mind has been working overtime which is never a good sign.

Suddenly I notice the gate has a latch on it, I try and pop it up with my nose, I am used to opening doors with handles at home so a latch should be easy. I jump up at it several times using my nose and paws and eventually the gate swings open and I'm in with the alpacas. They stare for a second with their huge eyes nearly popping out of their woolly heads. Then they start running away, I just want to introduce myself so I start to run after them howling. We do a few circles of the enclosure as I try to catch up with them. 'Wait for me! I only want to make friends! I give them my most friendly Hallooooooo.'

Mum and Aunt Julie hear the commotion and see me chasing the alpacas around the pen but there's nothing they can do as the alpacas are big and there are three of them. Then in a flash the alpacas are out through the open gate...... the chase is on!

Up to the top field, they have gone from a sedate trot to a canter and then into what an alpaca would call a gallop. The only thing which will stop them now is a Peruvian gaucho on a horse! I am in hot pursuit of them, I'd better follow them, at least someone will know where they have gone. We are still running full tilt up the field when I sense I have company its Dexter and Reicher! They have abandoned their tea and are both haring up the field after me. They must think alpaca chasing is much more exciting than kibble.

Then I hear Uncle Craig shouting and he is waving but I can't understand what he is saying. Is that something about a tent. I soon realise what he means, as we reach the top field, there is a family having a barbecue. They have set up their tent just out of sight at the top of the field. Aunt Julie and Uncle Craig don't just have a farm, they rent out their field to families to go camping.

The family look surprised to see a convoy of animals and humans run through their lovely peaceful holiday spot.

Three runaway galloping alpacas chased by three dogs, chased by four humans chasing the three dogs, chasing the three alpacas.

I think Mum said afterwards that it was collectively called 'Mayhem'. Murph would have loved it, I told her about how I caused Mayhem when I saw her but she said she's done it many times before and it's no big deal. But I do think she was secretly a bit jealous!

The family look terrified at the oncoming Alpacas and retreat to their tent. The Alpacas run close to the tent and carry on running across to the next field. At this point I am feeling very out of puff, my legs are tired but my nose is never tired, it starts twitching, what is that amazing smell? I stop dead in my tracks, what's this?

Sausages……abandoned sausages. They've even put them on a plate…..I LOVE sausages….. they are even better than chasing alpacas. I soon find out that my cousins Dexter and Reicher love sausages too. There are plenty to go round, and sometimes I don't mind sharing.

Mum, Dad, Uncle Craig and Aunt Julie must love alpaca chasing as they are still running after them. They won't mind if we continue our investigations of the barbecue. We sniff around a bit more and find some cooked chicken in a tray under the barbecue, we may as well eat that as well. Barbecues are great fun, we licked every plate clean. It's a good thing they didn't have a pattern, or we would have licked that off too. A few minutes later with full tummies and feeling tired, just like the Three Amigo's we head back to the farmhouse thirsty from our exploits, in search of a nice bowl of water. There is still no sign of the family with the tent, they must have gone to bed early.

We sit by the door waiting to go in for the longest time then I give a little howl as I see in the distance everyone returning over the top of the hill with the Alpacas. I thought everyone would be happy after having so much fun with the alpaca chasing but it doesn't seem that way. We decide to stay put as I have a feeling that Mum's not happy with me.

The alpacas are put to bed and us dogs are put to bed without any food! Uncle Craig orders free Dominos pizzas for the family in the tent and opens a bottle of ale for himself. As us dogs snooze the evening away we hear bottles popping and everyone laughing. It's nice when our humans see the funny side of things. It usually means that we are forgiven. It's been a great day all round, the best fun I've had for the longest time and I can't wait to tell Murph all about it.

Chapter 17. The Macedonian Mole Hound – Murph.

   Hi, Murph here, It's about time that Milly let me get a word in.
   Now she's told you all about her exploits with the alpacas. I wish I had been there to see it. I hope Milly takes me to meet them soon. I could give them a run for their money.
    At about the same time, my Mum decided that I needed to have an education. My Mum thinks that dogs should have good manners and do as they are told. That way, if we go to the pub or to visit family I will know how to conduct myself without being a bit of a disgrace like I was at Uncle Giles house in Cornwall.
   After hearing about Milly and the incident with the alpacas, Mum did some research, she had been taking me to obedience classes for a while and I am really good at walking to heel and sit and stay. I was not so good at 'Murph come.' but with lots of practice I am getting better. It's not that I don't listen, or that I don't want to go back. It's just that there are so many other things to be investigated. My nose tells me I must follow other scents, find what's at the end of a trail. Mum says it's the hound in me. I think she understands, but she's not very pleased

when I high tail it across the Common in search of my next big adventure.

My Mum can whistle through her fingers, she has worked on a farm and her whistle can be heard miles away. I can hear it, loud and clear with my ears, but my nose tells me that I should sniff for just a few minutes longer.

I also love to investigate mole hills. Moles are funny little creatures. They live under the ground in tunnels with little dens at the end. Sometimes when they are making their tunnels they pile all the spare earth on the surface in a little hill. I love mole hills! Mr Mole makes them in a line, following where he has made his tunnel. I am very good at listening to the ground. If I listen carefully I can tell where Mr Mole is working. Then I sniff along the line of his burrow and find the mole hill that he is digging under. Then I pounce, and I use my huge paws to dig for all I'm worth. I dig, dig, dig and I rip the ground up with my teeth and I try to get to Mr Mole. I have never found him, but I know he is there. Mum has usually put my lead back on before I get to his house. Sometimes my Mum is a bit of a spoilsport.

Anyway, after my adventures in Cornwall, and Millys exploits at agility, Mum did some digging online, and decided it would be good to try a thing called Man-trailing.

I had no idea what it was, but it sounded like fun. Only thing was, I had to wear a harness and a long line. Mum had bought me a harness when I was a puppy. I have grown a bit since then and the first time we went, it was a bit tight. I already had a long line, as Mum doesn't always trust me off lead, due to my love of following a smell.

It was a Sunday, Mum put me in the back of the car and we drove to a place called Cefn Cribwr, (I think you say it kevin crib oor) it's not too far from our village. We stopped in a car park on a nature reserve. The sign had pictures of rabbits and squirrels and ducks. This must be fun.

There were several other cars there all with dogs in the back. All sorts of dogs, but all with one thing in Common, dogs who liked to sniff things out.

Mum got out and chatted with some of the other owners and we waited for a while, and then a big van arrived with a man called Thomas in it, he was our instructor.

'Have you all brought a scent article.' He asked.

Mum produced an old sock which she said she had worn to the gym several times. Other owners produced hairbrushes or scarves or a glove. Something personal that they had worn or used.

'Have you got your dog's favourite reward.' I knew Mum had garlic sausage with her, I had been able to smell it since we got in the car. Ham is nice, but I can ignore Ham. garlic sausage on the other hand...... I adore garlic sausage. Some people say that dogs shouldn't eat garlic. I say everything in moderation. Mum says that Police dogs are given garlic on their food to stop them getting worms. I'm with Mum on the theory of garlic. Mum produces a box holding a chopped-up piece of Polish sausage.... Yum.

Thomas took the register and booked us all in and took all our names, he scratched my ear and said I was a lovely looking dog, then he asked what breed I was. Mum said that she called me a Macedonian Mole Hound. Thomas didn't get that she was joking. He said he had never seen one of those before. Then he said I looked like a very strong dog, and he hoped that Mum could keep up with me. My Mum is pretty fit, she will be fine.

Then Thomas gave our instructions.

Harnesses on...and I would be on a 15-foot line. We would work one dog at a time and our humans would take it in turns to hide from the tracking dog.

This really does sound like very good fun.

Eventually it was my turn. A lady gave Mum her scent article, it was a hairbrush. Mum put it on the path in front of me and let me sniff it. She had given this lady my box of garlic sausage and the lady had gone into the woodland around us and was hidden somewhere, now all I had to do was find her and all the garlic sausage would be mine. But where was she.

I put my nose to the hairbrush and breathed in deeply, then I pushed it with my snout and breathed in again. Then I sniffed around and found the direction where the smell had gone.

Thomas told Mum to give me the instruction. 'Trail!'
Mum gave the command. 'Murph, trail!'

I was off........I did not need telling twice, up the path, out to the full length of my line, through some bushes, around a corner.... Mum was running to keep up. I LOVE THIS..... Then the scent stopped. I stopped, I sniffed around a bit and there it was again on the other side of a puddle. 'Found you.' I let out a howl, just like the dog in that film that Dad was watching the other day. 'The Hound of the Baskervilles.'

There she was, hidden behind a tree. I did what Mum had told me to do when I ask for treats. I sat and I looked at the lady, when she didn't give me my reward instantly I woofed at her!

Then she gave me two pieces of garlic sausage and Mum gave me loads of praise. Thomas said I was a natural.

Well, I am a Macedonian Mole Hound after all! With a bit of Segugio Italiano thrown in for good measure.

At the end of the morning after I had found another three people I was given a certificate with my name on and had my picture taken for Thomas's website.

Mum signed me up to go man-trailing again in a few weeks' time.

I know she told Geraldine about it and I hoped that Milly might join us, but our next session was on a day when Millys humans were in work, so I went with Mum on my own.

This time we met up with the other trackers at a place called Kenfig Pool nature reserve. The car park was huge and there were lots of other more experienced trailing dogs sitting with their humans in the backs of their cars. I had my proficiency certificate and I was now ready to start proper training. Thomas said that the trails would be longer and more testing and that the target human might be hidden amongst other people. He told Mum that I might need a few goes to get the hang of it, but with a nose like mine I was sure I would do well.

Everything was going really swimmingly, I had completed two trails and found a man hiding under a table in the picnic area. Then I had found a lady hiding in the toilets. This was really difficult as the toilets smelled nearly as strongly as the lady did. Then we had lunch and after lunch we were going to do a long trail through the sand hills.

I was to do the first section. This time I was on a longer line, farther in front of Mum. I was really enjoying myself, this was all too easy for me. I saw Thomas whisper something to my target, a young man whose dog was a Springer Spaniel called Milo. His name was Jeff. Jeff gave Mum his scent article, an old glove he had been wearing, then he ran off into the sand hills and we waited. Then Thomas said we could start.

I leapt straight out to the extent of my track line and headed off down the sandy path into the dunes. We had been trailing for about five minutes when the scent stopped. I checked and doubled back, then I went forward again. The target, Jeff, had doubled back on himself, he wasn't fooling me. I did a quick double back and in the twitch of a nostril picked up the scent again going towards a pond. Then I saw Jeff hiding in the bushes on the other side of the pond. I launched myself at him, expecting garlic sausage and tummy rubs. I landed in the pond with a big SPLOOSH. Then I heard a scream and a yell behind me it was Mum shouting. 'Murph! STOP!'

As I turned I realised that my track line had wound itself around Mums legs and my leap into the bushes had pulled them out from under her. I stopped just in time to see Mums feet leaving the floor as she fell head over teapot and landed heavily on her bottom on the path.

Thomas and the other trackers rushed to see if she was alright. Mum got up and dusted herself down, she's tough, is my Mum, she wouldn't admit it if she was a bit bruised!

What is it with noses, mine took over and I sat in front of Jeff, soaking wet and covered in pond slime waving my paw at him for my reward.

Mum laughed, as she said, nothing more than her dignity was injured. She told me I had done amazingly and that I deserved my treats. She gave me the rest of the garlic sausage. But we did not go man trailing again.

Mum did tell Geraldine a few weeks later that it was a shame that Thomas had had to close his business. That she enjoyed taking me trailing but the nearest school was now in Gloucester and that was a bit far even for a Macedonian Mole Hound.

My photo and my certificate are still proudly displayed on the sideboard. Maybe one day I can go again and maybe I can take Milly with me. She can take one of Geraldines slippers and maybe a pack of Marks and Spencer's ham as her rewards.

Chapter 18. Social Media - Murph.

Milly and I are now 4 years old. Mum says I'm old enough to know better, I'm sure Millys humans say the same. We still live within sniffing distance of each other, and I still break the rules sometimes. Well, that is what rules are for isn't it? I never break rule 1, that is the one about wee and poo in the house. The other rules are flexible. I try to confine my excavations to the patch of weeds in the corner of the garden, the bit which mum calls her wildflower patch. I resist the temptation to dig up the lawn or the flowers. This seems to be a good arrangement.

My nose still gets me into trouble and mum says I have two sets of ears, one set which can hear the fridge door opening from half a mile away, and one set which completely ignores any reasonable request for obedience. Mum is now an expert at reading my mind, she knows when my nose is in charge and then I know that I will be on my long line for the whole of my walk. When I meet up with Milly she has much the same arrangement. It must be in our genes.

Now and again our humans chat about the place which rescued us from the dump. It is called Pawpers in the Ruff. Millys mum says that it takes an awful lot of human money to buy kibble for the dogs like us that they rescue. It takes even more to pay the vets bills to make some of the dogs better.

Marija and Ivana try and save all the dogs they can. They believe that every dog has a chance. Sometimes the dogs themselves seem to have given up, but then with a bit of love and warmth, food and treatment from Ivica the vet, they get better. Then Pawpers will try and find them a home.

They have a thing called a Facebook Page where they post pictures of the dogs who would love to go to forever homes like ours. They also have one where us dogs who are already here can keep in touch. It's called the Family page because after all, we are all one big Pawpers family. Only last week Mum and Geraldine were chatting in the car, me and Milly were in our space at the back, pulling faces at the little girl in the car behind us. Making her laugh. We were on our way to the beach.

They were chatting about the other dogs who came over on the van with us. It seems like so long ago now.

Mum was driving and Geraldine was reading the Pawpers family page.

'Oh, look Mags, do you remember Loakee, his dad has posted some pictures, gosh he got really big, he's been on all sorts of adventures, look there's pictures of him camping with his family and barking at the sheep in Wales'.

'Mum please don't look at the pictures, we might crash.' Milly and I brace ourselves as my Mum negotiates the roundabout.

'Oh look, Loakee is watching the rugby World Cup! Milly did that too with Rob.' Geraldine keeps talking.

'So did Murph, we watched it in the house.' My mum joined in.

'You Pawpers seem to have a lot in Common. Oh, and look, Loakee has even met up with his brother Charlie, I bet that was chaos. Isn't it great that we can all keep in touch!'

We turn into the car park and I can smell the sea, and more to the point I can smell the bait boxes the anglers carry with them.

Milly is starting to get excited, we both howl to get out of the car. It's a little, low level *ooooopen the dooooor'* howl.

'Be patient you two, leads on while we get down onto the sand.' Geraldine teases us while my Mum goes for a car park ticket. Then the hatch back door goes up and we both sit nicely and wait for our leads to be clipped on. Then out we jump, down the concrete ramp where they launch the boats and out onto the sand.

The tide is out, the sea seems so far away, but we can soon run there, come on Milly, let's go. I pull hard on my lead and Mum says, 'Okay then, SIT!'

I do as I'm told; I know that freedom comes next.

Leads off, we run as fast as we can towards the sea. Milly can run faster than me, but I can run for longer.

Mum has the ball chucker and my tennis ball, Geraldine has Millys rubber ball. I don't mind playing chase, but I'm not good at retrieving. Something always distracts me.

Mum throws my tennis ball into the sea, right in over the waves. I run after it, I love the water, I love jumping over the waves and I am a really good swimmer.

There's the ball, I've got it. It's deep here, my paws don't touch the floor. Milly doesn't really like to be out of her depth. There she is waiting for me. I open my mouth to say hello and I drop the ball, just in time for Milly to steal it, then she's off being a GOOD GIRL and taking it back to our mums. She knows there will be cheese or ham as a reward. Well she's not having all of it! I chase after her, barking, *'wait for meeeee Milly.'*

Mum says it's the luckiest picture she's ever taken. Two dogs running out of the sea, one carrying an old tennis ball, both having the best of times.

As we walk along the beach, Mum and Geraldine are still looking at that thing called Facebook. They still play with us, throwing the ball into the waves. Talking in between times, how do they manage to do all these things all at the same time. My Dad says it's called multitasking – it's a thing that Dads can't do.

'Look there's a message from Dobby and some pictures, gosh he's a handsome boy. He loves the beach as well. His Mum says that he was very nervous to start with but has come on loads. Here read this'.

Even though Dobby was around 5 months when we got him, he was nervous of most things - last year's holiday we couldn't get him into the lodge or to walk on the decking.

We had to slide him along the floor to get him in to the vets or groomers and he wouldn't go near any shop doors.
He wouldn't walk across a bridge or go near water.
This year he walked straight into the lodge, he walks straight into the vets, he walks into the groomers reluctantly - can't blame him.
Plays in the puddles and doesn't think too much about where he's walking.
Beautiful boy.

Our mums sit down on a big rock looking out to sea while Milly and I make the most of our freedom. We explore the rock pools and stick our noses into the very smelly piles of seaweed. I manage to find an old fish head and carry it behind a rock so that Mum can't see me having a sneaky munch on something nasty. Well she thinks its nasty, I think it has Michelin Stars.

Geraldine is still scrolling through the Family page.

'Look Mags, Daisy and Charlie, doesn't Charlie look huge and he is so hairy. They were on the same transport as our two. Charlie only has 3 paws, bless him, but it doesn't stop him at all. Oh look, they've been away on holidays abroad, France and Spain, aren't they lucky. Charlie has passed his sniffer dog exams just like Murph, and look he loves to dig holes as well, and swim. He and Daisy certainly fell on their feet.'

I can see my Mum looking over Geraldines shoulder.

'Who are those two?' She asks, they were on our van as well weren't they.

'That's Nela and Nika, what a cute photo. Oh and there is Otis we mustn't forget Otis.'

'Is that William? I think his owner changed his name, he is called Kenzie now. My word he looks so much like Murph, only he's white, and he has that crazy patch over his eye.'

'Well they all look as if they are having the best lives. I'm glad our two are as well. Pawpers work so hard to do their best for the dogs.'

'Oh Mags look what Loakee's Dad has written about him. He seems to have loads in Common with our girls. He was called Pavlos in Macedonia so they changed his name To Loakee. Look he is part Segugio Italiano as well, and Mountain dog, it's no wonder he grew so big. His Dad says he's 35kg now. That's the same size as Milly and Murph. Read this Mags it's wonderful'.

Loakee is the most affectionate lad with us humans and greets everyone who walks through the front door with cries of " I've missed you " and big swinging bum shakes. He loves his dog walkers 2 days a week where he's bundled in a van with 12 other dogs of all shapes sizes and breeds to run off lead in rural Bedfordshire. In confusing us humans he's not the best, off lead so must remain on lead around the local park with his random negative reaction towards other dogs. At home he patrols the garden for feline cat burglars who always outwit him. He loves the occasional treat of cheese and chorizo and comes running at the rustle of a crisp packet or popping lid of a food container. Would we ever swap this big bundle of love for a day off.....no way! He is ours and he's a special boy who completes our family and happiness.

'Now where are our two? Up to no good I expect.'

Milly and I have been sitting behind the rock, listening in. We heard it all. It's great to catch up with news of old friends.

'There they are!' My Mum reaches into her pocket for a piece of garlic sausage. Milly and I flop down on the sand, it's cool and smells of the sea. We both love the beach.

'Have you seen this?' My Mum is showing Geraldine something on her phone. 'Little Bruno, he is all the way up in Scotland. He lives with a family and shares his life with a Dachshund called Dennis, he says he has to walk everywhere which he loves, and that Dennis has taught him how to dig using one paw and balancing on his nose. He looks really happy.'

I gave a big huff and thumped my tail on the sand, Milly did too. Looks like we all found love and forever homes.

'Come on lazy dogs! One more swim and then we'll go home.' Mum and Geraldine are off their rock and heading for the waves. The tide is on its way in, soon the beach will be covered by the sea. I have one more jump in the surf and Milly has a bit of a paddle, then we all head back for the car.

My Mum doesn't much like 'The Socials' but it's a great way to catch up with old friends.

There was only one bit of sad news that day. After we got home Marija posted that Old Misha had crossed over the Rainbow Bridge. I wasn't certain what that meant, but everyone was adding sad Emoji's so it can't be a good thing.

Now that's a funny word for a dog to learn, *Emoji.*

I think it means that Misha finally went for his Long Sleep. He was a wise old dog, Ivica and Marija will miss him, and I think I will miss him too.

Chapter 19. The Rainbow Bridge – Milly.

I was only months old when I made the long trip from the dumps of Macedonia with my sister Murph. We were scared leaving all that we had ever known and being put into a cage in the van but at the same time we were happy that we were still together. After the journey we were picked up by our new humans and taken to our forever homes. I was so sad to say goodbye to Murph but already felt loved as I was taken into my new home by my lovely Mum Geraldine.

I couldn't believe my eyes when I saw another dog! I was overcome with excitement and ran over to say '*Hi, Im Milly, who are you?*' I found out later her name was Layla and she was a lot older than me. Layla sniffed me but didn't seem too excited to see me. I started following her around a lot and watched everything that she did and tried to copy her. The biggest thing I had to learn living in a house was to go outside to do my wees and poos like Layla. I had a few accidents but soon picked it up and I even learned how to open the door with my paws to let myself out.

At first Layla didn't know what to make of me as I had so much energy running here and there with my new ball, spilling my water bowl, jumping on the sofa, nipping Laylas paws, barking at the doorbell and ripping my blanket. I also used to try and eat Laylas food as I was used to fighting for food on the rubbish dump as we didn't know when we would eat next. I soon learned that living in a forever home meant that you ALWAYS had food and never went hungry.

    Eventually I settled down and Layla became my doggy foster mother. She taught me not to be afraid of the waves at the beach, not to be scared travelling in Dads car, how to behave on the lead and meeting other dogs. I saw her give her paw for treats and to sit and lie down when told. All these things I learned from her. I loved snuggling down for afternoon naps with Layla and cuddling up at night time with her big heavy paw resting reassuringly on my shoulder. I was so happy in my new home, I felt like the luckiest dog in the world, loved and safe. I finally found my happy ever after.

    Time flew by, I had my first birthday the following March. I was getting to be a big girl now. I noticed around this time that Layla didn't want to play as much and she would sleep a lot, Mum said she was over 12 years old which is very old in dog years. She was a very old lady. Layla was very slow on our walks so me and Mum had to walk slower for Layla to keep up and not feel left behind. I was feeling sad for her and for me as I so wanted to play with her.

Mum always took my favourite ball out so I had plenty of time running around whilst Layla plodded along and just watched me having the best time wearing myself out. A few weeks after my first birthday Layla became very unwell, she was struggling to walk, and Dad took her to the vet to have her checked out. Layla had to have an X-ray, that's a picture the vet takes of your insides to see what is wrong. A few days later Mum had a phone call to say it wasn't good news. Mum was crying and she came over to me to give me a hug. Mum then went and sat on the floor next to Layla and cuddled her for a very long time. I didn't understand everything but I knew things weren't right, something was very wrong with Layla.

A few more weeks passed and Layla was more and more tired and didn't want to go out for a walk, I sensed that she was in a lot of pain. Then one day Mum was crying a lot and I didn't know why, I tried to make her feel better by giving her my paw and licking her hand but she still looked sad. The next day Mum said I was going to Nan and Grandpas for the afternoon, I was so excited. Normally Layla comes too but she was sleeping, so I went over to her and touched her paw with mine and tried to nuzzle her to wake her up. I was hoping she would wake and come to visit the grandparents with me like she always did. She just opened her eyes and looked at me and went straight back to sleep. Poor Layla she looked so old and so sad.

'Don't worry Layla I will be back soon, and we can snuggle, and when you are better we can go to the beach and jump over the waves together, you'll see'! Love you Layla, see you when I get back.'

I had the best time at the grandparents! I played ball in the garden, watched the goldfish in the pond, a walk in the field and some special treats. I was napping when Dad came to collect me. He spoke to nan and she was wiping tears from her eyes and grandpa gave her a hug. Dad looked sad too, I didn't know Dads cried. But mine does. I sat in the back of the car and felt sad too but I didn't know why.

We were soon home and I jumped out of the car excited to see Layla, I ran in to tell her I was back but she wasn't there. Where is she? I need to tell her all about my visit to the grandparents. I ran out to the kitchen and then the garden but she was nowhere to be seen. Something didn't feel right. Mum came downstairs, she was crying A LOT, she gave me the tightest hug. '

'Oh Milly.' she said. 'Layla's gone, I'm so sorry, you are going to miss her so much I know. Layla was very old and unwell and was in a lot of pain so she had to go over the Rainbow Bridge'.

Over the Rainbow Bridge? Laylas gone without me somewhere I've never been. I ran to the window and looked out for the longest time, waiting for her to come back so she could tell me about her adventure over the Rainbow Bridge. It sounded like a lovely place to go. Eventually I got fed up of looking out the window and I had my food and settled down for the night. I slept next to Mum and Dads bed that night and heard Mum crying herself to sleep.

The next morning I woke up early and ran downstairs to see if Layla was back but she wasn't. Mum came down looking sad and put Laylas blanket in my bed, I sniffed it and I could smell Layla and it made me feel a bit sad as she still wasn't there. I laid on her blanket and waited and waited. I looked out of the window and kept watch for the next few days. Waiting for her to come back from her trip to the Rainbow Bridge, but she never came.

Sometimes on our trips to the beach I see a German Shepherd that looks just like Layla and he reminds me of her, I always run up to him and bark and say, 'have *you seen her, have you seen Layla.*' He just looks at me down his long nose, like German Shepherds do. He never says anything, but he looks sad too. As if he knows. Maybe they were friends. Maybe he misses her but can't talk about it. I miss her so much. It's been 3 years and I still see him and still think of Layla, but now I know she's never coming back.

Mum told me that they had taken Layla to the beach that day when I went to the grandparents. It was her last special walk with them, and then they took her home and she fell asleep and went to the Rainbow Bridge, where all old dogs go. I don't really understand how she can go somewhere when she's sleeping, but Mum said Laylas happy there and that she's waiting for me, but it will be a long time before I go.

I sometimes dream about her especially being in the sea and jumping over the waves with her and making me feel safe. I didn't have Layla in my life for very long but I still love her with all my heart. I hope she will be waiting for me when it's my time to cross the Rainbow Bridge.

Maybe I'll talk to Murph about the Rainbow Bridge on our next walk. She might know where it is. Her Mum might even have it on her Sat Nav. Murph's Mum knows where everywhere is. I'd just like to go to that bridge and see where she went. Not to stay, just to say goodbye properly and make sure she's okay. She even forgot to pack her blanket, but I will look after it for her. Goodbye Layla sleep tight.

Chapter 20. Sisters in the Ruff - Milly and Murph.

    Hi, Murph here, It's Sunday morning, it's very early, I can smell that it's going to be a lovely sunny day. The sun is starting to stream in through my window. I yawn and stretch and roll onto my back on my bed. Maybe I should close my eyes and have another half an hour snooze. I love a good snooze. I can hear Dad moving around upstairs, the human toilet flushes. I still can't see why they don't wee and poo outside like we have to!
    He's coming down the stairs, into the kitchen, I hear the water tap running, then the sound of the kettle being switched on. Now he's opening the refrigerator. He must be making my breakfast. He opens my bedroom door. Then I hear him banging the fork on my bowl and calling.
    'Good morning Murph. Come and get it!'
    I turn myself the right way up and trot across the dining room to the kitchen. Yes! Breakfast is served, and there's scraps on the top. Dad always gives me bits of leftover meat from the fridge. It's chicken this morning. Yummy.

'I think Mum has a surprise for you today, she's getting up already. I think she's taking you to do something you really enjoy.'

Dad always talks to me when he's in the kitchen making his coffee and I'm eating my brekky.

I can hear Mum coming down the stairs, she is wearing her old jeans and a sweatshirt, she is dressed for a walk.

'Make me a coffee while I get her stuff together please.' Mum asks Dad. 'Has she had her breakfast? '

'All done. She's raring to go, aren't you Murph?' My humans are a good team.

Mum disappears out to the car. I can hear her putting things in the boot, I trot to the big window to see if I can see what's happening. Then I go and check the front door, maybe it's open. If it is then I might go and investigate.

When I was very little I sneaked out of the front door. The cat from across the road was sitting on its windowsill. It dared me to chase it, so I did. I jumped over all the garden walls in the street, woofing and making hunting noises with the cat always one garden ahead of me. I am better at hunting now. That cat wouldn't take liberties with me now. Mum was not amused, she had to come and collect me from a lady called Sylvia's garden. Sylvia lives next door. She's lovely and very kind, but she wasn't happy that I'd trampled all over her begonias.

I didn't catch the cat, it sat just out of reach and teased me for days after. I told it that it was a very childish cat and it needed to get out more. It must have listened to me, because it disappeared. It's human was very upset when it was found, she brought it home wrapped in a blanket. She told my Mum it had crossed the Rainbow Bridge. It was trying to get home from the park when it forgot to look both ways to cross the road. I miss that cat, just a bit.

I don't understand this Rainbow Bridge thing. It seems to be like the Long Sleep Old Misha told us about. But he didn't say anything about rainbows. Maybe I'll chat to Milly about it.

Today, the front door is closed, Mum won't make that mistake again. She comes back in and finishes her coffee, then we are off!

'Come on Murph, let's go. Let's find Milly!'

At the mention of my sister, my ears prick up, I'm going out with my sister Milly, but where?

I jump into the back of the car, Mum clips me on to my seatbelt and shuts the tailgate. There is a big lumpy bag wedged in the corner, and the water bowl has been packed. What's going on? Where are we going? Then, the engine starts and we are off. I'm looking out of the back window, waiting to see my sister. It won't be long, she doesn't live far away.

Meanwhile in Millys house:
Hi, Milly here, why is Mum getting me up early, it's Sunday, I want a lie in, and treats, and tummy rubs from the kids. Mum is very excited. I hope she's not too excited, 'cos that usually means singing.

'Come on Milly, let's get going. Maggie's outside with Murph in the car.'

The tailgate is open and I jump in with my sister. Greetings and ear licking over, we settle down for a chat. We haven't had a good tail wag for a while. Murph is eager to catch up on our news.

'Hey Milly, can you believe that we are nearly five years old. In a few months it will be what our humans call our 'Gotcha Birthday.' The anniversary of when they picked us up from Sheffield after that long journey from where we were born. We have been in Wales for four whole years.'

'Does that make us Welsh then Murph?'

'Mum says that it makes us middle aged in doggie years. Did you know that five years for a dog is about thirty-two of their human years.'

'That's what Geraldine told me as well, Murph. She was teasing Dad Rob, telling him that we were both getting old.'

'Don't worry Milly, your humans are younger than mine, and I suppose that we will all get older together. As long as we all still want to go for a walk and they remember to feed us that will be okay.' Typical Murph always thinking of walks and food.

'But are we Welsh, Murph?'

'What do you dream about Milly? I dream about chasing squirrels on the Common and running through the waves and along the beach. But sometimes I do still dream of the dump.'

'Me too, Murph, sometimes I can still smell the rubbish, and the rotting food, the old tin cans and burning plastic. Do you think there are still dogs there Murph? Old Alpha must have crossed the Rainbow Bridge by now.'

'What is this Rainbow Bridge, all the humans talk about it and when they do they all get really sad. Yet they say it leads to a wonderful place, what do you think Milly? Is it like the Severn Bridge? If it is then Alpha must be coming to join us in Wales, and Layla must have gone to England 'cos that's where the Severn Bridge goes! It joins Wales and England.'

'Oh Murph, don't be silly, it's not that sort of bridge. Geraldine says that it's the bridge to a beautiful place where all us dogs will get to eventually.'

'Well, that's it then! We are already there, we crossed the bridge into the beautiful place called Wales, see I'm right, aren't I. They've painted the Severn Bridge in Rainbow colours and we are on the beautiful side! I nudged Milly hard and bounced up and down making the dog barrier rattle.

'Quiet in the back you two, what's all the racket about?' My Mum turned the radio up louder. I hoped our Mums weren't going to start singing.

'But what about England, Murph, that's a beautiful place too. There are loads of beautiful places we haven't seen and they are all on the other side of the bridge. No you are wrong about the bridge, and anyway it's called the Prince of Wales Bridge, it says so on the sign!' Milly was being a know it all.

'Maybe we could go on an adventure one day and find the Rainbow Bridge. Just to see it, I don't want to see the other side of it yet, but we could pack plenty of treats and see if we can find Misha and our doggie mother. You could give Layla her blanket, she must be missing it!'

'Oh Murph, do you think we could.'

'If we are together we can do anything.'

'I would like that. Just to see them all one more time. Do you think there are any dogs left on the dump Murph?'

'There will always be dogs on the dump, Milly. As long as there are humans who treat us like rubbish. We are two of the lucky ones. When we were two tiny scraps of life, only a few days old, we were rescued by the wonderful humans at Pawpers in the Ruff.' I lay down with a big huff.

'I think that as long as we remember them and dream of them, we will always be a bit Northern Macedonian. Just a bit. And Dad Rob says they don't have a bad football team!' Milly watches far too much television.

'I think we are just a little bit of both, we should never forget our roots. We are part Sarplaninac like Misha and part Italian Hound like our mother - Segugio Italiano. I think it says on that test mum sent off to find out. I still think of Misha sometimes. He was so old and so wise!'

We felt the car slow down and turn into a small carpark in some woods, I was sure I'd been here before, but when I was little. All thoughts of the Rainbow Bridge disappeared in the anticipation of another adventure.

'Hey Murph, here we are! Look there's other dogs; we can bottom sniff! Oh, and there's Tom! Tom from Mutz 'n' Strutz. I knew they would sort it; I heard my Mum on the phone to yours.' Milly was really excited.

'Did they pack our harnesses and our long leads, Milly?' I could already smell all sorts of lovely smells; I was excited too.

'I think I'm lying on them Murph, calm down can't you, you have your big hairy bottom in the water bowl.'

'Never mind that, get your best nose on Milly, we are going Man-trailing! Man-trailing is just the best. I knew Mum would bring me again and I know you are going to love it. It's the best thing for noses ever!

On our best behaviour we sat in the back of our car and waited for our turn. Sisters, so alike but so different.

All dogs love to dream, when we have had our tea and our tummies are full, and our humans are doing human things. You might see our paws moving and hear us woof in our sleep. We may be chasing rabbits or squirrels across fields and up trees.

Me and Milly have come a long way since we were rescued. Now we have other dreams to make our paws twitch and our cheeks puff. We have dreams of running on the beach, splashing in the waves. Chasing squirrels through the woods and rolling in the grass on the Common. Sometimes we still dream of the dump, we think of old Misha - might he have been our father? In our prayers we thank Ivana and Marija and Ivica the vet and Pamela who raises the money to keep the centre going, and we think of all the ones who were not so fortunate as us.

Milly and Murph together forever - it's just how it had to be.

THE END.

A bit about Pawpers in the Ruff.

Our mission is to provide lifesaving care, rescue and rehoming to stray dogs in Macedonia.

Pawpers in the Ruff helps the dumped and abused dogs in Macedonia. Many of the dogs in our care have only ever known life on the streets or living within a city or on a dump. Together we can show them a happy and loved life. Since starting, we have rescued over 1,500 dogs and neutered and released hundreds more.

Our main focus is helping the dogs on the city dump. We provide as much food and healthcare as our resources allow. This work is so tough, we have to make some really hard choices about who we save and who we have to leave behind. The conditions here are really harsh, it is not a safe environment and there is very little food or shelter. We see some really hard things, but the money you kindly donate helps us turn these lost souls into happy, healthy and loved dogs.

The spay and neuter project.

After a lot of time spent at the dump, we quickly came to the conclusion that rescuing dogs and puppies wasn't a long-term solution. We needed to stop more and more puppies being born into these cruel conditions. So we decided to start a programme to spay and neuter as many dogs as we could. However, it's not that easy.

Some dogs are wild and need anaesthetics to be captured and some are not healthy enough for surgery. Sometimes they might need placing in care for a month before they are well enough. If we do not have the funds to keep them after surgery, they will be released back to the dump.

How to adopt a dog.

Please see the link on our website: pawpersintheruff.com for details of the adoption process.

Notes and Acknowledgements.

This book has been written from the perspective of two amazing rescue dogs from Northern Macedonia. Milly and Murph. Without their input it would not have been possible.

Their story is told in their own words with a little help from their families. I would also like to thank Geraldine Barrett-James for providing the 'Milly' chapters.

Photographs and pen pictures have been provided and are produced with the consent of the owners of the other rescue dogs who travelled to the UK in September 2021.

I would also like to thank all Milly and Murph's friends in our village who may have gotten a mention in the book together with their dogs, rescue or otherwise.

There are many charitable and voluntary bodies both in the UK and abroad who spend their valuable time and resources on the welfare of stray and abandoned dogs and other animals. As my husband asked at the beginning of this journey. 'Why not adopt a dog from the UK?' The answer to that is. 'Why not adopt a dog from the UK.'
In our case it was just a case of timing, and falling in love with a cute puppy who later grew to be 35kgs of fun.

There are many lovely dogs in the rescue centres of the world, all waiting to find a forever home. If you are considering getting a dog, then seriously consider adopting. Give a rescue dog a chance.

If you enjoyed our story and have bought our book please take time to visit our Facebook page. PAWPERS IN THE RUFF, and our website:

pawpersintheruff.com

There you can see more of the great work these unpaid humans do. You might consider making a regular donation to PAWPERS through PayPal: pitr103@outlook.com or even give one of our friends a forever home. You won't regret it.

The Route Map.

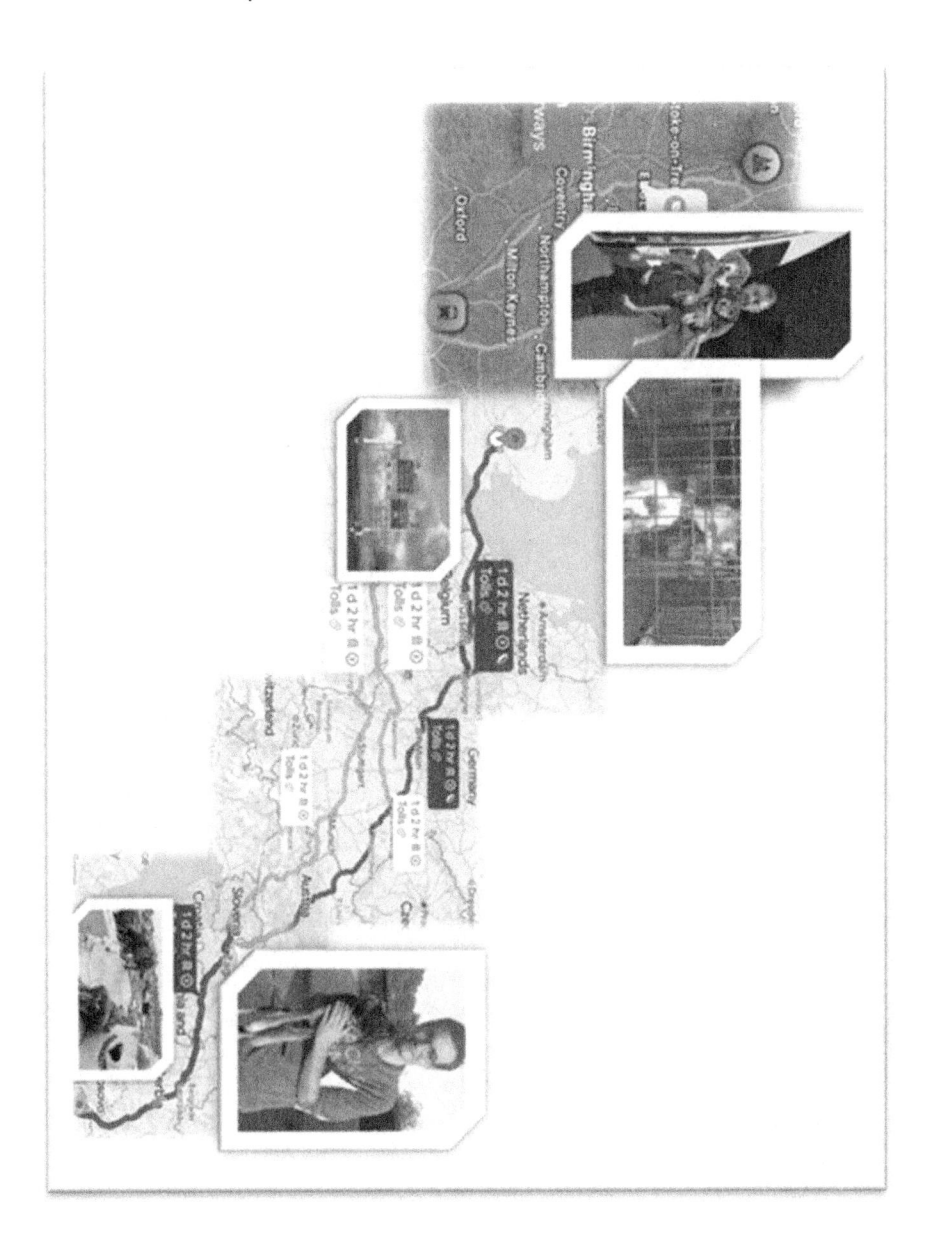

Meet the Gang.

Copyright.

The right of Maggie Jenkins to be identified as the author of this work has been asserted by her in accordance with the Copyright, Designs and Patents Act 1988. All characters and events in this publication are fictitious and any resemblance to real persons, living or dead, is purely coincidental.

All rights reserved. No part of this publication may be reproduced, stored in a retrieval system or transmitted in any form or by any means without the prior permission in writing of the publisher, nor be otherwise circulated in any form of binding or cover other than that in which it is published without a similar condition, including this condition, being imposed on the subsequent purchaser. A CIP catalogue record for this book is available from the British Library. ISBN: 978293418343

Other novels by Maggie Jenkins.

Ginger Like Biscuits – The Adventures of a Welsh Mountain Pony.

Cassandra's Web – Karma follows on the Heels of Injustice

The Meredith Saga: The Journey of a family bound to the hills and mysticism of Wales. Follow their journey through time and history, romance, and warfare from The Battle of Crecy to who knows where.

Titles in series:

An Arrow Through Time

Bullets Through the Mist

Shadows and Subterfuge

Published through Amazon in paperback and Kindle.

The Author may be contacted by email: authormaggiej@gmail.com

Printed in Dunstable, United Kingdom